I0000336

Forensic Analytics

Steven M. Bragg

AccountingTools®

Copyright © 2025 by AccountingTools, Inc. All rights reserved.

Published by AccountingTools, Inc., Centennial, Colorado.

No part of this publication may be reproduced, stored in a retrieval system, or transmitted in any form or by any means, except as permitted under Section 107 or 108 of the 1976 United States Copyright Act, without the prior written permission of the Publisher. Requests to the Publisher for permission should be addressed to Steven M. Bragg, 6727 E. Fremont Place, Centennial, CO 80112.

Limit of Liability/Disclaimer of Warranty: While the publisher and author have used their best efforts in preparing this book, they make no representations or warranties with respect to the accuracy or completeness of the contents of this book and specifically disclaim any implied warranties of merchantability or fitness for a particular purpose. No warranty may be created or extended by written sales materials. The advice and strategies contained herein may not be suitable for your situation. You should consult with a professional where appropriate. Neither the publisher nor author shall be liable for any loss of profit or any other commercial damages, including but not limited to special, incidental, consequential, or other damages.

ISBN 978-1-64221-252-5

For more information about AccountingTools® products, visit our Web site at www.accountingtools.com.

Table of Contents

About the Author

Steven Bragg, CPA, has been the chief financial officer or controller of four companies, as well as a consulting manager at Ernst & Young. He received a master's degree in finance from Bentley College, an MBA from Babson College, and a Bachelor's degree in Economics from the University of Maine. He has been a two-time president of the Colorado Mountain Club, and is an avid alpine skier, mountain biker, and certified master diver. Mr. Bragg resides in Centennial, Colorado. He has written more than 300 books and courses, including *New Controller Guidebook*, *GAAP Guidebook*, and *Payroll Management*.

Steven maintains the accountingtools.com web site, which contains continuing professional education courses, the Accounting Best Practices podcast, and thousands of articles on accounting subjects.

Buy Additional AccountingTools Courses

AccountingTools offers more than 1,500 hours of CPE courses, with concentrations in accounting, auditing, finance, taxation, and ethics. Related courses that you might like include:

- Behavioral Forensics
- Fraud Examination
- Fraud Schemes
- How to Audit for Fraud

Go to accountingtools.com/cpe to view these additional courses.

AccountingTools®

Forensic Analytics

Introduction

The particular focus of this book is on the detection of *occupational fraud*, in which employees misuse or divert their employer's assets for personal gain. This type of fraud can be found anywhere in an organization, and can involve amounts large enough to bankrupt it. Given the financial impact of fraud, it makes sense for a business to engage in forensic analytics, which uses data analysis techniques to detect number anomalies that indicate the presence of fraud and errors. Otherwise, management is reduced to waiting for the occasional tip or just luck to detect fraud – which could take years, by which time the related losses could be substantial.

Forensic analytics provides a useful backstop to a company's normal system of detective and preventive controls, so that fraud situations can be uncovered that might otherwise never be found. It is particularly useful when tracking down smaller fraudulent transactions that are specifically intended to slide underneath the parameters of a company's control systems. For example, purchases for amounts less than $1,000 may not require a purchase order, while check payments under $10,000 do not require a second signature. Canny operators are aware of these control weaknesses, and specifically tailor their activities to not be detected. Fortunately, a well-constructed forensic analytics system improves the odds of spotting these transactions.

In this book, we describe the steps involved in a forensic analysis investigation, the process required to import data into Excel for further analysis, and the types of data analysis techniques that can then be conducted within Excel to locate anomalies.

Forensic Analytics Defined

Forensic analytics is a set of techniques used to discover patterns in a data set that can pinpoint the presence of fraudulent transactions. Examples of these techniques are:

- *Test for abnormal duplications*. Looks for expenditures in the same amount that recur an unusual number of times.
- *Test for round numbers*. Looks for unusual quantities of round numbers, which tend to be frequently used when creating fake transactions.
- *Test for outliers*. Looks for values that are well outside the amount of a normal transaction.
- *Test for growth spurts*. Looks for instances in which the growth rate of a series of numbers is unusually high, which could indicate the presence of a rapidly-increasing case of fraud.
- *Tests for cubic volume*. Looks for numerical values of physical items, where the cubic volume of those items in a company's records exceeds the actual storage volume of the business.

We discuss these techniques, as well as other analysis tools, later in this book.

Common Characteristics of Fraudulent Transactions

A fraudulent transaction could involve any amount, and so might initially appear to be impossible to spot, especially since auditors tend to focus their work on larger values. However, a fraud event has historically proven to have one or more of the following characteristics, at which forensic analytics can be targeted:

- Amounts deviating from Benford's Law
- Amounts just outside of control thresholds
- Amounts that are large outliers
- Duplicate amounts
- Numbers involving strong growth rates on a trend line
- Round numbers

As we will see, a well-constructed analysis has a good chance of extracting fraudulent transactions from a data set, even when they may be hidden by thousands of other transactions.

Forensic Analysis Steps

The following steps should be followed to plan for, conduct, and evaluate a forensic analytics procedure, where the intent is to identify numeric anomalies that may indicate the presence of fraud:

1. *Set objectives.* Decide upon what type of fraud the analysis is intended to uncover, such as the presence of bribery payments to customers or the use of company procurement cards for personal expenditures.
2. *Select data.* Choose the type of data that is most likely to be relevant to the analysis. For example, one might select operational data or financial data, current or historical data, and so on.
3. *Determine the testing tool.* Pick the testing tool that is best suited to the stated objective, and obtain the needed software. In this book, we assume that Excel is being used.
4. *Access and prepare the associated data.* Obtain access to the data, convert it into a readable format, engage in data scrubbing as needed, and load it into the analysis software. Part of this step involves consideration of the reliability of the data, especially if the parties potentially committing fraud can access and alter the data. Data scrubbing involves spotting incorrect or inaccurate data and replacing or modifying it as needed. We cover data importing and scrubbing in the following section.

EXAMPLE

An analyst wants to compare office supplies transactions across business units, to see if there are any purchasing anomalies. Doing so calls for some data preparation, since each of the business units accounts for its office supplies under a different account number. Also, some business units purchase in bulk at longer intervals than others that do so on a more incremental basis. Finally, some business units place large, varied orders with a single office supplies distributor, while others buy from a range of suppliers. These variables may call for some scrubbing of the data to make it more comparable across business units.

5. *Conduct the test*. If the test uncovers issues that warrant further action, plan and perform procedures on these issues. If the initial results of the procedure indicate that it requires revision, then make the necessary changes and reiterate the process, changing any data groupings and employing data filtering as needed.
6. *Evaluate the results*. Decide whether the objectives of the test have been achieved. If not, use other tests or data sources that are more likely to achieve the objectives.
7. *Present the outcome*. Develop conclusions from the tests and present them to the target audience. For example, the outcome might be an executive summary, a list of suspicious transactions, a discussion of the total financial impact, a summary, and recommendations for how to proceed.

EXAMPLE

Company management is concerned that the firm's procurement cards are being misused, and authorizes a project to investigate this possibility. The internal auditing staff sets an objective of determining whether there are any instances of card misuse. It requests a download of the past 12 months of data on card purchases from the credit card company, and uses Excel to conduct the following analyses:

- Sort the purchases in declining numerical order. This spotlights 15 purchases made for more than $10,000, which greatly exceed the $1,000 policy limit on card purchases.
- Sort the purchases by supplier and then aggregate these purchases by day. This spotlights 12 instances in which card users asked suppliers to split invoices into smaller amounts and charge them through separately, in order to get under the maximum policy limit on card purchases.
- Compare the suppliers to a list of approved suppliers. This highlights 20 cases where purchases were made from unapproved suppliers, four of which were for personal purchases.

Excel Data Importing and Scrubbing

Excel is the main tool used by forensic accountants. It is heavily employed by them on a day-to-day basis, so their general familiarity with it makes it easier to adapt for forensic analytics tests. The first step in using Excel is importing data into it and then scrubbing the data to make it more usable for forensic analysis. We describe how to do so in detail in the following sub-sections. By taking these steps, the accountant has a much cleaner set of data from which to conduct forensic analytics activities, which are described later in the book.

Data Imports

Excel is most useful when it can import masses of data from outside sources for analysis. The software incorporates a number of importing routines that allow for the automated importing of many text file formats, using the Open command that is accessed through the File tab on the Excel ribbon. The Open dialog box specifies that the file types noted in the following exhibit can be opened.

File Types Opened by Excel

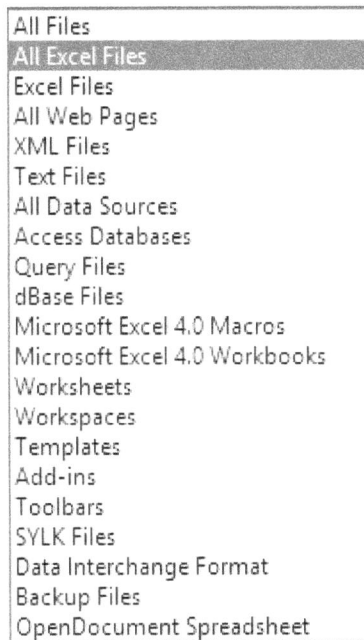

```
All Files
All Excel Files
Excel Files
All Web Pages
XML Files
Text Files
All Data Sources
Access Databases
Query Files
dBase Files
Microsoft Excel 4.0 Macros
Microsoft Excel 4.0 Workbooks
Worksheets
Workspaces
Templates
Add-ins
Toolbars
SYLK Files
Data Interchange Format
Backup Files
OpenDocument Spreadsheet
```

Besides opening files from all previous versions of Excel, the software can also open the last item on the preceding list, which is an OpenDocument Spreadsheet; this is an open software format for spreadsheets, charts, presentations, and word processing documents that is used by a number of "open" software programs.

Other items of note in the preceding exhibit are the ability to open several database file formats, such as Access, Query, and dBase, as well as many types of text files, including the following two commonly-used formats:

- *CSV.* This file type contains comma-separated values, where each line of the file is a data record, and each record consists of one or more fields that are separated by commas.
- *TXT.* This file type is used for a text file, and is used by a variety of text editors. A carriage return is used to insert row breaks.

Excel will need to install a process, known as a data import wizard, to import TXT files. To activate this wizard, select the File tab on the Excel ribbon and click on the Options command in the left sidebar. This will bring up the Excel Options dialog box. Click on the Data option from the left sidebar of that box, which brings up a set of data import wizard selection options, as noted in the following exhibit. Click on the checkbox for the "From Text (Legacy)" option, which is highlighted in the following exhibit with a red arrow. Checking this selection will add a menu item to the Data commands in the Excel ribbon, which will be needed for our next step.

Data Import Wizard Selection Options

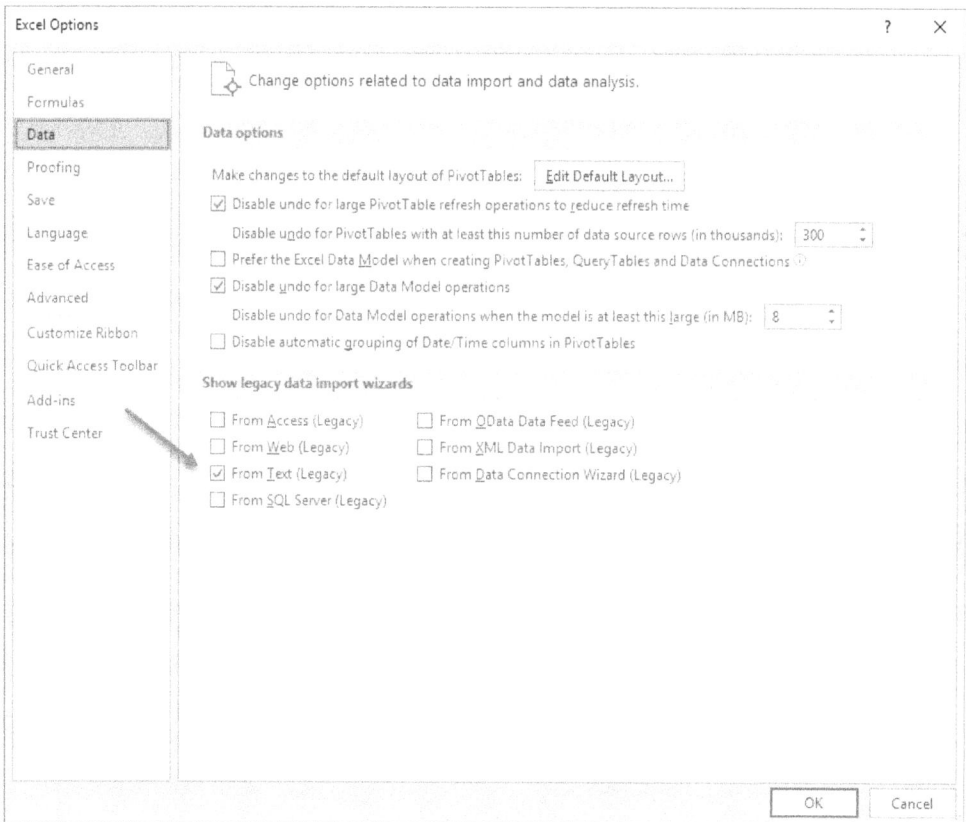

We will use the preceding text import wizard to import a text file into Excel. The contents of this text file appear in the following exhibit, where the revenue, expenses, and profit for each month are separated by commas.

TXT File Contents

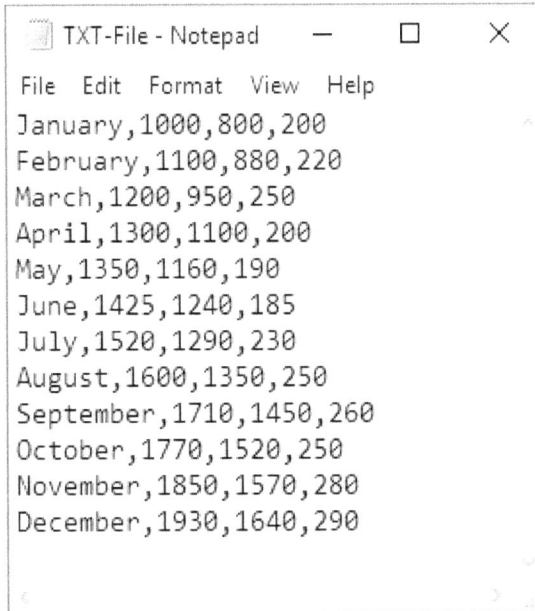

```
TXT-File - Notepad        —    □    ×

File  Edit  Format  View  Help
January,1000,800,200
February,1100,880,220
March,1200,950,250
April,1300,1100,200
May,1350,1160,190
June,1425,1240,185
July,1520,1290,230
August,1600,1350,250
September,1710,1450,260
October,1770,1520,250
November,1850,1570,280
December,1930,1640,290
```

To import this file into Excel, select the Data tab on the Excel ribbon, pick the Get Data command, and click on the Legacy Wizards option from the dropdown menu. The following exhibit shows the location of these commands.

Legacy Wizard Command

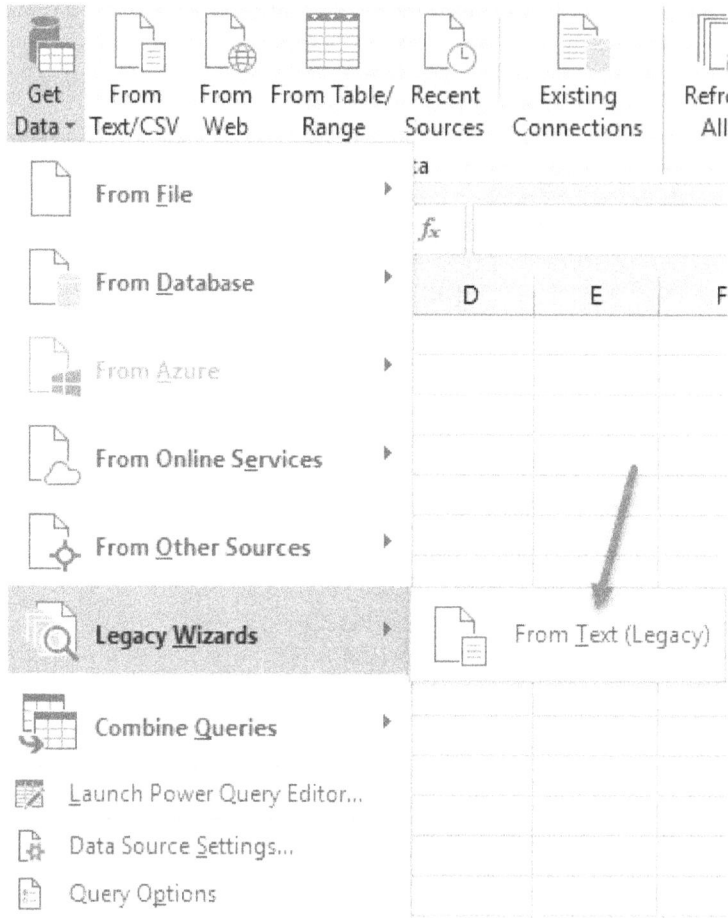

Click on the From Text (Legacy) option, navigate to the location of the TXT file, and click on the Import button. Doing so brings up the first of three Text Import Wizard dialog boxes, the first of which appears in the following exhibit. Since the data being imported is separated by commas, select the Delimited option within the dialog box (as highlighted in the exhibit with a red arrow). Then select the Next button to continue to the next page.

Text Import Wizard – Step 1

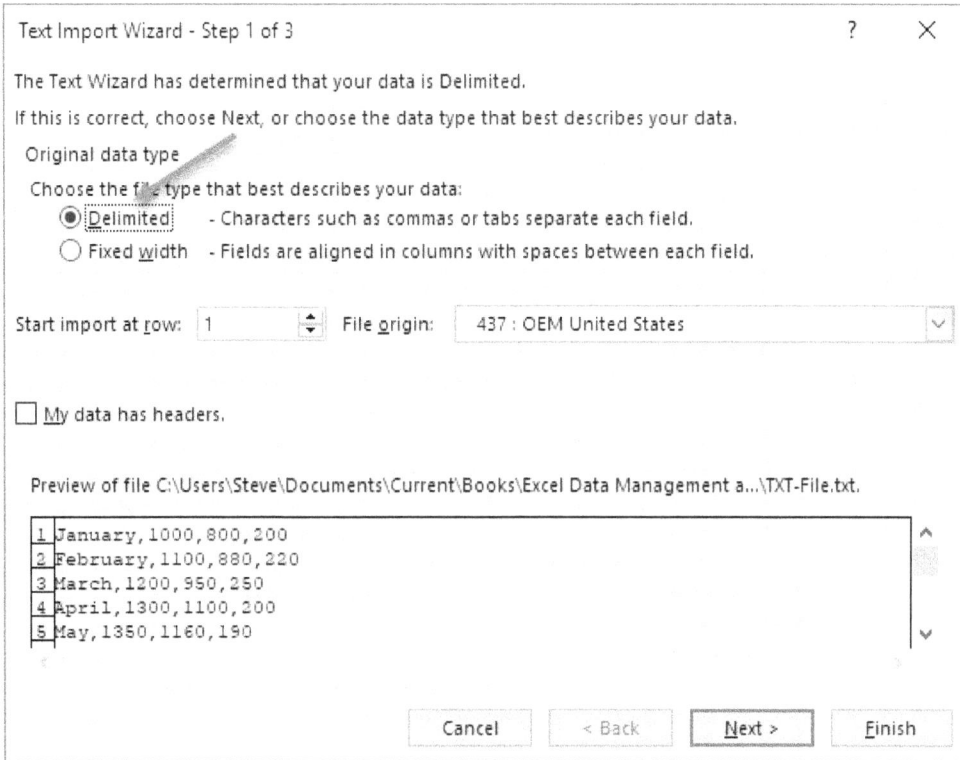

Text Import Wizard - Step 1 of 3   ?   ✕

The Text Wizard has determined that your data is Delimited.

If this is correct, choose Next, or choose the data type that best describes your data.

Original data type

Choose the file type that best describes your data:

   ⦿ Delimited   - Characters such as commas or tabs separate each field.

   ◯ Fixed width   - Fields are aligned in columns with spaces between each field.

Start import at row: 1   ▲▼   File origin: 437 : OEM United States   ⌄

☐ My data has headers.

Preview of file C:\Users\Steve\Documents\Current\Books\Excel Data Management a...\TXT-File.txt.

```
1 January,1000,800,200
2 February,1100,880,220
3 March,1200,950,250
4 April,1300,1100,200
5 May,1350,1160,190
```

Cancel   < Back   Next >   Finish

The second dialog box for the wizard appears in the following exhibit. The only entry to make is to select the Comma option from the range of available delimiters on the left side of the screen. Doing so presents a data preview near the bottom of the box that shows how the data in the text file will appear in Excel. We have noted the comma delimiter option with an arrow, and surrounded the data preview section with a red box.

Text Import Wizard – Step 2

Click the Finish button in the lower right corner of the dialog box. Doing so brings up the Import Data dialog box, which appears in the following exhibit. In this box, state where the data is to be put in the receiving worksheet. By default, Excel assumes that it will appear beginning in cell A1.

Import Data

Import Data   ?   ✕

Select how you want to view this data in your workbook.
- ▦   Table
- ▦   PivotTable Report
- ▦   PivotChart
- ▦   Only Create Connection

Where do you want to put the data?
- ⦿ Existing worksheet:

  =A1| ⬆

- ◯ New worksheet

☐ Add this data to the Data Model

Properties...   OK   Cancel

The resulting data import appears in the following exhibit, where the import began in cell A1 (since we did not alter the default value in the Import Data dialog box). You can see that the original comma delimiters have been eliminated, and were used to parse the data strings and record their component parts into different cells.

Imported Data

	A	B	C	D
1	January	1000	800	200
2	February	1100	880	220
3	March	1200	950	250
4	April	1300	1100	200
5	May	1350	1160	190
6	June	1425	1240	185
7	July	1520	1290	230
8	August	1600	1350	250
9	September	1710	1450	260
10	October	1770	1520	250
11	November	1850	1570	280
12	December	1930	1640	290

The advantage of using one of these import wizards is that they can be quite effective at parsing data in a consistent manner.

A much cruder alternative is to simply copy from the source document and paste it into Excel by accessing the Home tab on the Excel ribbon, selecting the Paste command from the ribbon, and using the Paste Special command. If we were to do this with the preceding text file, the outcome would be as shown in the following exhibit, where the data is entered into Excel, but it has not been parsed into separate cells. This type of data transfer will clearly require a substantial amount of additional cleanup work before the data can be used.

Pasted Data without Parsing

	A
1	January,1000,800,200
2	February,1100,880,220
3	March,1200,950,250
4	April,1300,1100,200
5	May,1350,1160,190
6	June,1425,1240,185
7	July,1520,1290,230
8	August,1600,1350,250
9	September,1710,1450,260
10	October,1770,1520,250
11	November,1850,1570,280
12	December,1930,1640,290

Data Cleanup

It is quite possible that collected data requires cleaning before it can be analyzed. Excel has several useful functions that can be used to ensure that imported data conforms to user requirements, after which analysis can begin. We describe these functions next.

Duplicate Row Removal

When data imports are coming from multiple sources, there is a good chance that some of the data will be repeated, which means that there will be duplicate rows. The Remove Duplicates tool can be used to delete these duplicates. To access the command, select the Data tab on the Excel ribbon and then pick the Remove Duplicates command, located within the Data Tools cluster of commands. Doing so brings up the dialog box that appears in the following exhibit.

Remove Duplicates Dialog Box

To delete duplicate values, select one or more columns that contain duplicates.

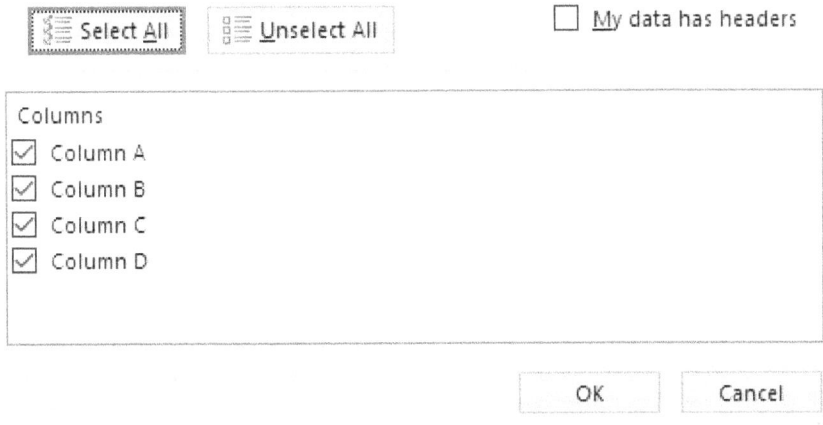

⬛ Select All	⬛ Unselect All		☐ My data has headers

Columns
- ☑ Column A
- ☑ Column B
- ☑ Column C
- ☑ Column D

OK   Cancel

This box lists all columns that contain data. Check the boxes for all columns that should be searched, which is usually all of them. When all columns are checked, Excel will only delete a row if *every* cell in that row is duplicated in another row. A case in which you might *not* want to check all rows is when there is a unique identifier in each row, such as a part number or an invoice number; in that case, deselect the column that contains the unique identifiers, or else Excel will not find any duplicate rows.

Then click on the OK button. Excel reviews the data and eliminates all duplicate rows, after which it returns a message similar to the one in the following exhibit, stating how many duplicates were removed. If the procedure appears to have been in error, use the Undo command in the upper left corner of the screen to undo the deletion.

Duplicate Row Elimination Message

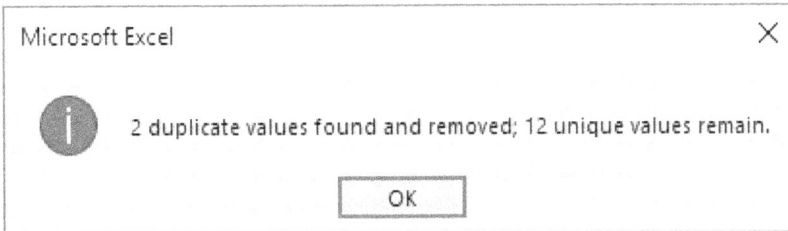

Microsoft Excel   ✕

ⓘ   2 duplicate values found and removed; 12 unique values remain.

OK

Note: Excel only considers values to be duplicates if they are formatted in exactly the same manner. Thus, it would not consider a value of $1,250.750 to be the same as $1,250.75 because of the extra decimal place in the first value, and so would not delete one of them as a duplicate. To keep this from happening, apply the same format to an entire column, so that formatting will not be the cause of a missed deletion.

Text Splitting

It is entirely possible that a data import will result in some values being mashed together into a single column, as noted in the following example. For some reason, the data import process was unable to parse the incoming values into different columns. In the exhibit, note how each string of data has been stored in a single cell within Column A.

Unparsed Data

	A
1	January 500 32 17 1
2	February 620 50 16 2
3	March 700 62 13 3
4	April 483 51 10 1
5	May 572 40 16 4
6	June 913 50 10 5
7	July 605 74 13 5
8	August 850 66 16 6
9	September 519 48 15 6
10	October 490 69 23 2
11	November 388 54 10 3
12	December 851 65 17 5

The situation can be dealt with by using the Text to Columns command. To use it, follow these steps:

1. Make sure that a sufficient number of columns to the immediate right of the subject column are empty, since the Text to Columns command will store the results of the operation in those columns. In the preceding exhibit, five empty columns would be needed.
2. Select the data that will be parsed, which in our example would mean highlighting the range A1 to A12.
3. Select the Data tab on the Excel ribbon, look for the Data Tools group of commands, and pick the Text to Columns command.
4. The Convert Text to Columns dialog box appears. It asks you to select whether there are commas separating the data or whether fields are aligned in columns with spaces between each field (which is the case for the preceding exhibit). As noted with the red arrow, we have selected the second option. Excel needs one of these selections in order to properly parse the data. Then click on the Next button at the bottom of the box.

Convert Text to Columns Wizard – Step 1

Convert Text to Columns Wizard - Step 1 of 3   ?   ✕

The Text Wizard has determined that your data is Fixed Width.

If this is correct, choose Next, or choose the data type that best describes your data.

Original data type

Choose the file type that best describes your data:

  ○ Delimited   - Characters such as commas or tabs separate each field.

  ⦿ Fixed width - Fields are aligned in columns with spaces between each field.

Preview of selected data:

```
1 January    500  32  17  1
2 February   620  50  16  2
3 March      700  62  13  3
4 April      483  51  10  1
5 May        572  40  16  4
```

Cancel   < Back   Next >   Finish

5. The second of the text conversion dialog boxes appears, as noted in the following exhibit. A series of column breaks appear in the lower left corner of the dialog box. You can create, delete, or move these break lines, as described in the box, thereby altering how the data will be parsed. Then click on the Next button at the bottom of the box.

Convert Text to Columns Wizard – Step 2

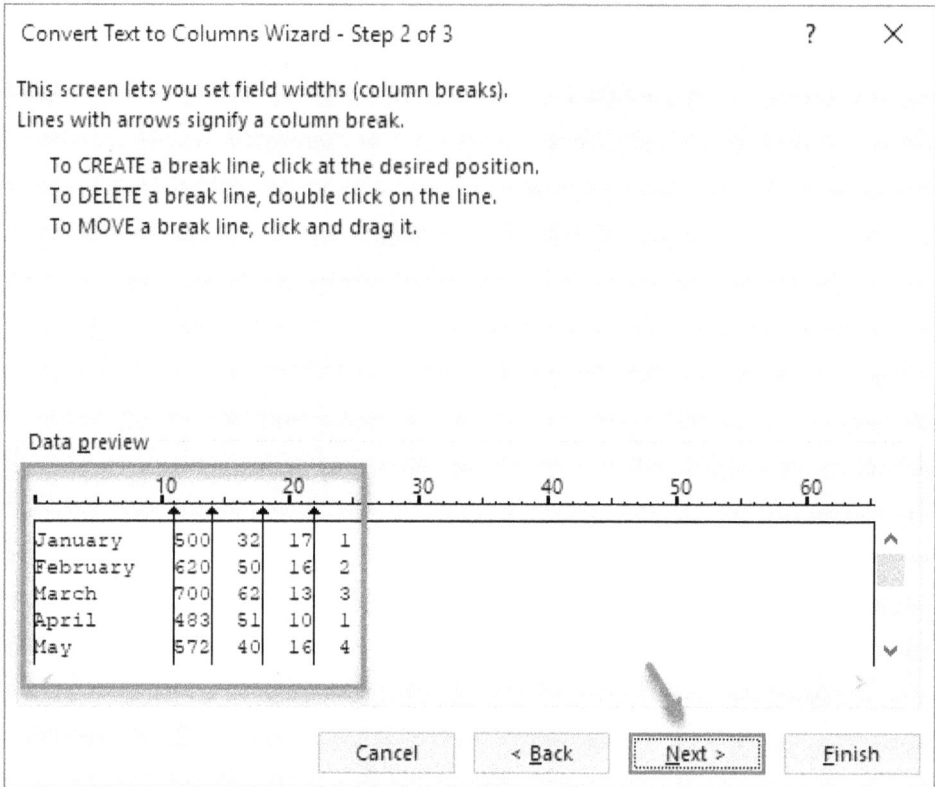

Convert Text to Columns Wizard - Step 2 of 3   ?   ✕

This screen lets you set field widths (column breaks).
Lines with arrows signify a column break.

    To CREATE a break line, click at the desired position.
    To DELETE a break line, double click on the line.
    To MOVE a break line, click and drag it.

Data preview

```
          10        20      30      40      50      60
January   500  32  17  1
February  620  50  16  2
March     700  62  13  3
April     483  51  10  1
May       572  40  16  4
```

    Cancel   < Back   Next >   Finish

6. The third and last of the text conversion dialog boxes appears, as noted in the following exhibit. This one involves clicking on each of the columns in the lower left corner of the screen and specifying the formatting to be applied. In the exhibit, we have specified text formatting for the first column and general formatting for everything else. Then click on the Finish button to trigger the parsing.

Convert Text to Columns – Step 3

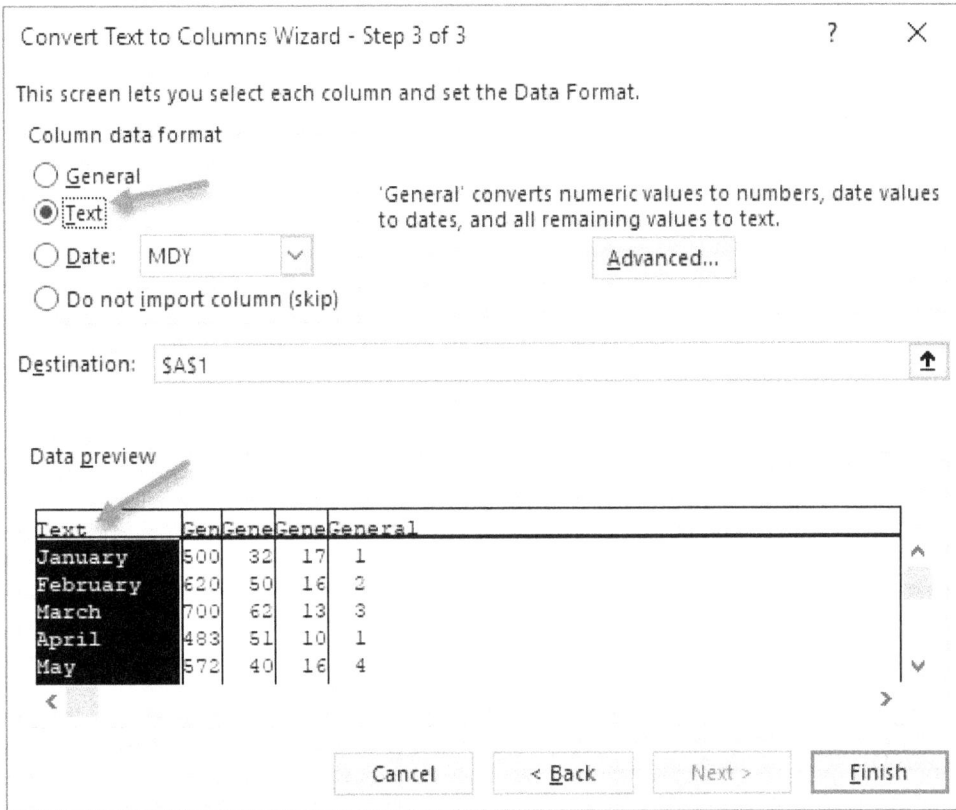

7. The final result appears in the following exhibit, where the initial text string has been broken apart and recorded in separate columns. The values in Columns B through E have been formatted as numbers, and so can be subjected to any number of additional analyses with Excel's formulas and functions.

Text Parsing Final Results

	A	B	C	D	E
1	January	500	32	17	1
2	February	620	50	16	2
3	March	700	62	13	3
4	April	483	51	10	1
5	May	572	40	16	4
6	June	913	50	10	5
7	July	605	74	13	5
8	August	850	66	16	6
9	September	519	48	15	6
10	October	490	69	23	2
11	November	388	54	10	3
12	December	851	65	17	5

Flash Fill

There may be cases in which the data being imported into Excel cannot be parsed, because it does not have handy delimiters, such as commas or spaces. In these situations, the Flash Fill command might be a useful alternative. This command is used to scan through an existing data set to recognize patterns, and then extract the relevant data and copy it into a different column. To use it, enter in the column adjacent to the data series a few correct answers for what you want to extract. For example, in the following exhibit, we entered Markus and Steven in cells B1 and B2, and then clicked on the Flash Fill command within the Data tab of the Excel ribbon. Excel compared the desired outcomes to the positions of these names within the data strings in Column A, and concluded that we were looking for just the first name of each person. It then automatically extracted the first names from the remaining names in Column A and copied them into the remaining adjacent cells in Column B. We used the same approach in Columns C and D, entering the first two names in each column; Excel then realized that we wanted to extract the middle and last names from Column A, and accordingly copied them into the appropriate columns. The result is a perfect parsing of the names in Column A, even though the names do not share common lengths.

Flash Fill Results

	A	B	C	D
1	Markus Hinton Andrews	Markus	Hinton	Andrews
2	Steven Ralph Jones	Steven	Ralph	Jones
3	Sarah Ruth Bingsley	Sarah	Ruth	Bingsley
4	Patricia Gina Caylor	Patricia	Gina	Caylor
5	Margarita Courtney Colon	Margarita	Courtney	Colon
6	Christy Amanda Taylor	Christy	Amanda	Taylor
7	Mario Ron Davis	Mario	Ron	Davis
8	Crystal Raquel Lagunte	Crystal	Raquel	Lagunte
9	Ryan Vernon Walters	Ryan	Vernon	Walters
10	Lana Ashley Armstrong	Lana	Ashley	Armstrong

The main downfall of the Flash Fill command is that it only works if the source data is consistent. For example, if some of the source names in the preceding example had lacked middle names, Flash Fill would have erroneously included several first names in the middle name column. We note these differences in the following column, where the middle names for two individuals from the preceding exhibit were extracted. The highlighted results indicate that the first name for both people was repeated in the column in which only middle names were to appear.

Erroneous Flash Fill Results

	A	B	C	D
1	Markus Hinton Andrews	Markus	Hinton	Andrews
2	Steven Ralph Jones	Steven	Ralph	Jones
3	Sarah Ruth Bingsley	Sarah	Ruth	Bingsley
4	Patricia Gina Caylor	Patricia	Gina	Caylor
5	Margarita Colon	Margarita	Margarita	Colon
6	Christy Amanda Taylor	Christy	Amanda	Taylor
7	Mario Davis	Mario	Mario	Davis
8	Crystal Raquel Lagunte	Crystal	Raquel	Lagunte
9	Ryan Vernon Walters	Ryan	Vernon	Walters
10	Lana Ashley Armstrong	Lana	Ashley	Armstrong

Case Changes

The text in a cell may not be formatted in the manner you want. There could be caps where lower case is desired, or vice versa. Excel provides three functions that can be used to address this issue. The UPPER function converts text to all upper case, while the LOWER function converts all text to lower case, and the PROPER function begins all words with upper case and converts all other letters to lower case. An example of all three functions appears in the following exhibit, where the original text is stated in cell A1, and cells A3, A4, and A5 are used to present the outcomes of the UPPER, LOWER, and PROPER functions, respectively, when they are applied to the original sentence.

Change Case Commands

	A	B
1	GO to paris for the AMAZING Food.	
2		
3	GO TO PARIS FOR THE AMAZING FOOD.	UPPER(A1)
4	go to paris for the amazing food.	LOWER(A1)
5	Go To Paris For The Amazing Food.	PROPER(A1)

Space Removal

Some text may include extra spaces that are not needed. These spaces may be located at the middle or end of a text string, or perhaps somewhere in between. If so, they can be eliminated by using the TRIM function, which will retain single spaces between words. In the following exhibit, we use the TRIM function to clean up text that has extra spaces in a number of locations within a cell. The formula is entered in Column C and appears in text form in Column D for explanatory reasons. The issue being cleaned up is stated in Column E.

Space Removal Example

	A	B	C	D	E
1					
2		Original Text	Revised Text	Function	Comments
3		Mildred	Mildred	=TRIM(B3)	Two spaces before the word
4		X Y Z	X Y Z	=TRIM(B4)	Excess spacing between the letters
5		John Q. Smith	John Q. Smith	=TRIM(B5)	Excess spacing between the names

Tip: A possible problem to deal with after using the preceding formulas to transform data is that the original text still exists alongside the transformed text. To copy the transformed data into the original source cells, highlight the range of cells containing formulas, press Ctrl-C to copy them, highlight the cells in which the original source text is located, go to the Paste command within the Home tab, and select the Paste Values option. The transformed data will now appear in place of the original text, and the formulas can be deleted.

Value Conversions

When importing data from multiple sources, it is possible that some of the values will be expressed in differing units of measure. For example, the fluid volume for one value might be expressed in ounces, while the fluid volume for another value might be expressed in liters. Similarly, one value might be in yards, and another in meters. Excel's CONVERT function can be used to convert values from one unit of measure to another. The arguments included in the CONVERT function are as follows:

=CONVERT (the value to be converted, the units for the value, the
units for the result)

For example, to convert feet to meters for a distance of 30 feet, the formula would be:

=CONVERT(30,"ft","m")

=9.144 meters

Some of the more common designations for units of measure appear in the following exhibit.

Conversion Codes

Celsius = "c"	Gram = "g"	Ounce = "oz"
Centimeter = "cm"	Inch = "in"	Quart = "qt"
Cup = "cup"	Kilometer = "km"	Tablespoon = "tbs"
Fahrenheit = "ft"	Liter = "l"	Teaspoon = "tsp"
Foot = "ft"	Meter = "m"	Ton = "ton"
Gallon = "gal"	Mile = "mi"	Yard = "yd"

Concatenation

Concatenation is the joining of character strings end-to-end. This can be accomplished rather easily in Excel with the ampersand (&) character. An obvious use is when the first name of a person is listed in one cell, while his last name is located in a different cell. To combine them, create a formula in a separate cell that uses the ampersand (&) character to indicate that the text in the cells should be joined. An example appears in the following exhibit, where we have also included a space between quote marks to indicate that a space should be inserted between the first and last names.

Sample Text Join Command

	A	B	C
1	First Name	Last Name	Combined Name
2	Harvey	Painter	=A2&" "&B2
3	Sarah	Strange	Sarah Strange
4	D'Angelo	Murphy	D'Angelo Murphy
5	Harold	Mills	Harold Mills
6	Christain	Templeton	Christain Templeton
7	Maura	Mao	Maura Mao
8	Javier	Butler	Javier Butler
9	Lori	Harris	Lori Harris
10	Theresa	Rixford	Theresa Rixford
11	Roxanne	Labita	Roxanne Labita

A variation on the concept is the TEXTJOIN command, which combines the text from multiple ranges, including a predetermined delimiter between each value that will be combined. The arguments included in the TEXTJOIN function are as follows:

=TEXTJOIN (The delimiter, ignore empty cells if TRUE, the text item to be joined,
the additional text item to be joined)

The delimiter could be a space, or a character (in which case it needs to be stated in quotes). An example of how the TEXTJOIN function can be used appears in the following exhibit, with the full formula stated in Column E. Note how the space delimiter inserts a space between the text coming from each of the source cells. Also, the TRUE setting is used to ignore all empty cells, which occur in Rows 2 and 3.

TEXTJOIN Command Usage

	A	B	C	D	E
1	Ms.	Martha	Masterson	Ms. Martha Masterson	=TEXTJOIN(" ",TRUE,A1,B1,C1)
2	Ms.	Kathy		Ms. Kathy	=TEXTJOIN(" ",TRUE,A2,B2,C2)
3	Ms.		Anderson	Ms. Anderson	=TEXTJOIN(" ",TRUE,A3,B3,C3)

Gap Filling

There may be cases in which a worksheet has gaps in the data, where an entry in one column is intended to apply to several subsequent rows. An example appears in the following exhibit, where the entry in Column A indicates that the sales in the next column will apply to that entry until a replacement entry is made. Thus, the unit sales by region are assumed to be for green widgets until replaced by the red widget indicator in Row 7, and so forth.

Gaps in the Data

	A	B	C	D
1				
2		Product	Region	Unit Sales
3		Green Widget	East region	10,000
4			North region	18,500
5			South region	6,700
6			West region	9,900
7		Red Widget	East region	5,400
8			North region	6,100
9			South region	8,000
10			West region	7,400
11		Purple Widget	East region	8,090
12			North region	9,870
13			South region	2,430
14			West region	5,600

This can be a problem when you intend to sort the rows, since this interferes with the inherent assumptions about which products were sold. One way to deal with the problem is to simply copy and paste the various entries in Column B into the empty spaces, but this is a time-consuming process. An alternative is to engage in a higher degree of automation, following these steps:

1. Highlight the range that contains gaps, which in the preceding exhibit was cells B3 through B14.
2. Select the Home tab, find the Editing group of commands within the Excel ribbon, and select the Find & Select command. Pick the Go to Special command from the resulting drop-down menu.
3. On the resulting Go to Special dialog box, select the Blanks option (as noted in the following exhibit) and click OK.

Go to Special Dialog Box

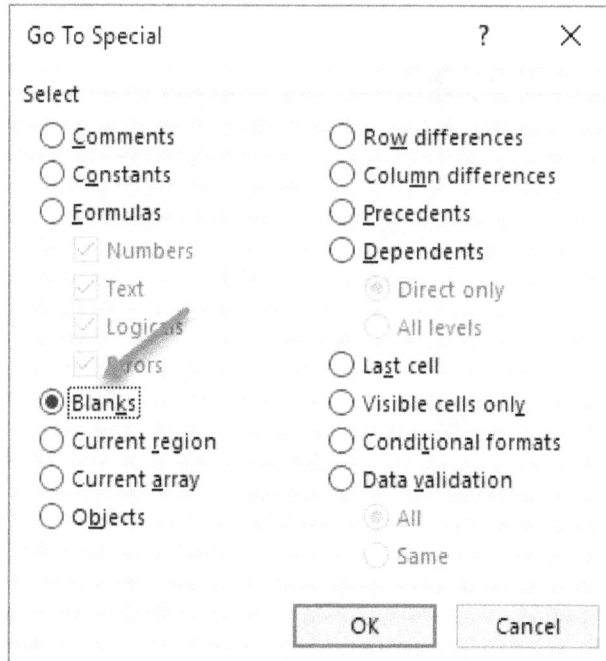

```
Go To Special                              ?    ✕

Select
   ○ Comments              ○ Row differences
   ○ Constants             ○ Column differences
   ○ Formulas              ○ Precedents
      ☑ Numbers            ○ Dependents
      ☑ Text                  ◉ Direct only
      ☑ Logicals              ○ All levels
      ☑ Errors             ○ Last cell
   ◉ Blanks                ○ Visible cells only
   ○ Current region        ○ Conditional formats
   ○ Current array         ○ Data validation
   ○ Objects                  ◉ All
                              ○ Same

              [    OK    ]    [  Cancel  ]
```

4. The layout of the spreadsheet changes to what appears in the following exhibit, where the blank cells are shaded, and cell B4 is the active cell. Go to the Formula bar near the top of the screen and enter an equal sign (=) followed by the address of the first cell that should be copied down, which in the example is B3. Then press Ctrl-Enter.

Highlighted Blank Fields

	A	B	C	D
1				
2		Product	Region	Unit Sales
3		Green Widget	East region	10,000
4			North region	18,500
5			South region	6,700
6			West region	9,900
7		Red Widget	East region	5,400
8			North region	6,100
9			South region	8,000
10			West region	7,400
11		Purple Widget	East region	8,090
12			North region	9,870
13			South region	2,430
14			West region	5,600

5. The result appears in the following exhibit, where all blanks have been filled in correctly, using the cells above them that already contained entries.

Completed Worksheet with Blanks Filled In

	A	B	C	D
1				
2		Product	Region	Unit Sales
3		Green Widget	East region	10,000
4		Green Widget	North region	18,500
5		Green Widget	South region	6,700
6		Green Widget	West region	9,900
7		Red Widget	East region	5,400
8		Red Widget	North region	6,100
9		Red Widget	South region	8,000
10		Red Widget	West region	7,400
11		Purple Widget	East region	8,090
12		Purple Widget	North region	9,870
13		Purple Widget	South region	2,430
14		Purple Widget	West region	5,600

6. The only remaining problem is that the formerly blank cells only contain formulas, not values. For example, cell B4 contains "=B3" rather than "Green Widget." To switch from formulas to values, highlight the range containing formulas and press Ctrl-C to copy it. Then go to the Paste command within the Home tab on the Excel ribbon and select the Paste Values option. The formula entries will now convert to values.

Spell Checking

The data in a worksheet is not necessarily spelled correctly. To conduct a spell check, press F7. Doing so will bring up the Spelling dialog box whenever Excel suspects that it has found an error. An alternative is to select the Review tab on the Excel ribbon and pick the Spelling command. To limit the spell check to just part of a worksheet, highlight the target area prior to picking the Spelling command.

Text Substitutions

There may be cases in which it is necessary to find and replace certain characters within the data. For example, the term "theatre" may appear in several places within a worksheet, and you want to replace it with the term "theater". The easiest way to do so is by picking the Find & Select command within the Home tab on the Excel ribbon and choosing the Replace option from the resulting drop-down menu. Doing so brings up the Find and Replace Dialog Box, which appears in the following exhibit. Simply enter the term to be replaced in the "Find what:" field, enter the replacement term in the "Replace with:" field, and then choose either the Replace All (to complete the replacement all at once) or the Replace (to replace one at a time) option to swap out the offending text.

Find and Replace Dialog Box

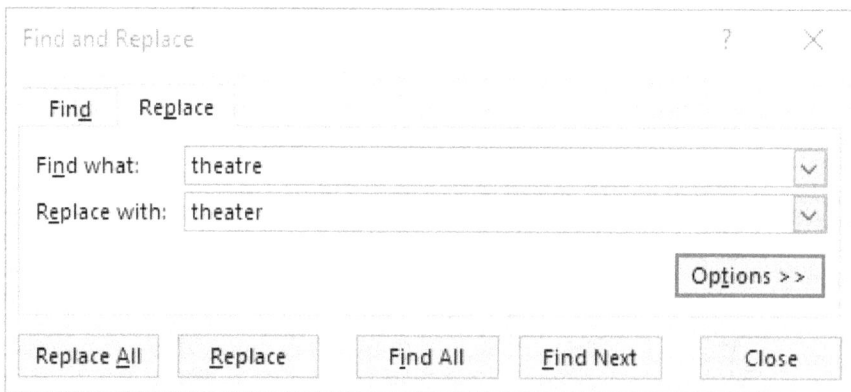

There may be other cases in which the search and replace activity calls for a more precise level of intervention. If so, use the SUBSTITUTE function, which contains the following arguments:

=SUBSTITUTE (the text for which characters will be substituted, the text to replace, the new replacement text, the occurrence of the old text to be replaced – this is optional)

For example, the text "December Sales" resides in cell A1. To roll this month designation forward to January, the SUBSTITUTE function would be:

=SUBSTITUTE(A1,"December","January")

A more complex example is when you have imported a thousand part numbers from a subsidiary that uses a hyphen between the segments of its part numbers. The corporate parent uses a colon (:) instead of a hyphen, so you need to swap out thousands of these characters. However, only the first hyphen encountered should be replaced with a colon. The following argument string could be used to do so:

=SUBSTITUTE(A1:A1000, "-",":",1)

The key ingredient in this argument string is the inclusion of the "1" at the end, which specifies that only the first instance of a hyphen that is encountered in each cell should be replaced with a colon.

Excel Forensic Analysis Techniques

In the following sub-sections, we discuss a number of analysis techniques that can be used to extract relevant information from an Excel data set, with the intent of detecting anomalies.

Missing Records Analysis

The first step in any data analysis process is to verify that the number of records imported into Excel matches the number of records from the data source. For example, if the auditor extracts a trial balance into Excel, then it would be reasonable to verify that the number of line items in Excel matches the number of trial balance line items. When there is a mismatch, and especially when the number of line items in Excel is lower than the record count in the source database, and *especially* when the download was provided by someone else, there is a fair possibility that records indicating the presence of fraud have been stripped from the download. For example, if the auditor asks the accounts payable manager for an Excel download of the payables register, and the number of line items provided is too low, the auditor would be well advised to find out what was in the missing line items.

Benford's Law

Benford's Law[1] states that, in a naturally occurring set of numbers, the smaller digits appear disproportionately more often as the leading digits. For example, in the number $17,421, the leading digit is 1. Zero is not allowed as a first digit, so there are nine possible first digits (1, 2, 3, 4, 5, 6, 7, 8, and 9). Also, the sign of a negative number is ignored, so that (for example) the first digit of the number -$237 is 2. Benford's original observations were compiled from a broad array of sources, including:

> ...the surface areas of 335 rivers, the sizes of 3259 US populations, 104 physical constants, 1800 molecular weights, 5000 entries from a mathematical handbook, 308 numbers contained in an issue of *Reader's Digest*, the street addresses of the first 342 persons listed in *American Men of Science* and 418 death rates.

The leading digits have the distribution shown in the following table, where the number 1 appears slightly more than 30% of the time as the leading digit, and the number 9 appears as the leading digit less than 5% of the time (which is a difference of 6x). Notice that Benford's Law also applies to numbers in the second position, but to a much lesser extent than for numbers in the first position.

Benford's Law Frequencies of Occurrence

Leading Digit	First Position in Number, Frequency of Occurrence	Second Position in Number, Frequency of Occurrence
0	--	1.19%
1	30.10%	1.14%
2	17.61%	1.09%
3	12.49%	1.04%
4	9.69%	1.00%
5	7.92%	0.97%
6	6.70%	0.93%
7	5.80%	0.90%
8	5.12%	0.88%
9	4.58%	0.85%

The same information is stated graphically in the following table.

---

[1] Named after the physicist Frank Benford, who published an article on this topic in 1938, "The Law of Anomalous Numbers."

Numeric Distribution in Benford's Law

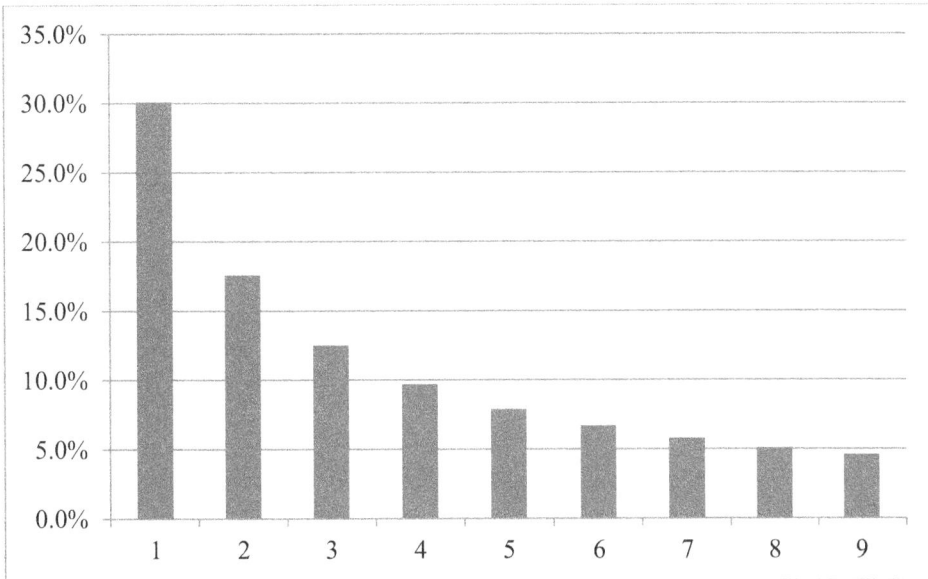

If all digits were to appear as the leading digit in a uniform manner, then each one would appear about 11.1% of the time. Since there is quite a disparity between the distributions stated in Benford's Law and what a uniform distribution of accounting data would indicate, this disparity can be used to locate instances of fraud.

The analysis involves calculating the distribution on the first digit in a series of numbers. If the distribution varies from the proportions indicated by Benford's Law, then it is *possible* that someone is engaged in fraud. The reason for the difference is that someone committing fraud will create randomly generated numbers, rather than following Benford's distribution. Additional investigation would be needed to ascertain whether fraud is actually present.

EXAMPLE

The data analysis team of Nuance Corporation wants to use Benford's Law as the basis for an examination of the invoices submitted to the company by its suppliers. The analysis is run for two suppliers, Supplier A and Supplier B, where the first digit is extracted from the total amount billed on each invoice. The results of the analysis are shown in the following two tables.

Supplier A Comparison to Benford's Law

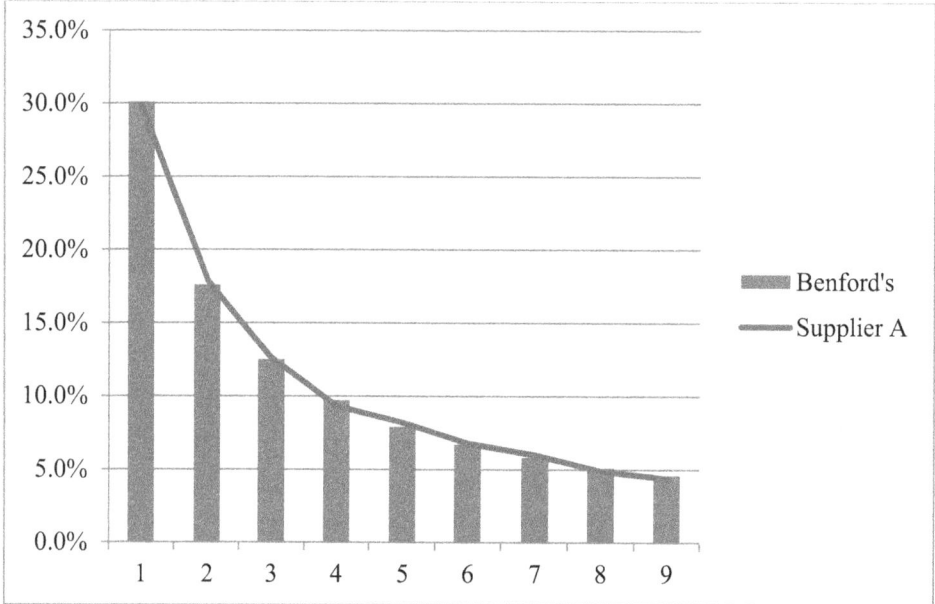

Supplier B Comparison to Benford's Law

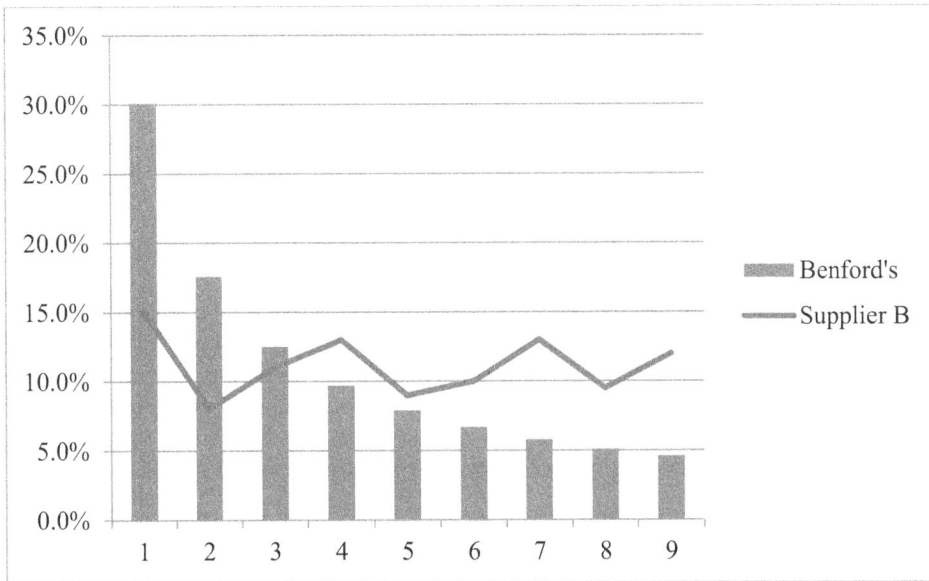

The analysis for Supplier A appears to be quite normal, with the actual numeric distribution closely following the proportions indicated by Benford's Law. This is not the case for Supplier B, where it appears that the supplier has been making up random numbers to be billed. The latter situation certainly calls for a more detailed review.

The use of a Benford-based analysis is especially useful in cases of financial statement reporting fraud, where an otherwise-canny group of managers makes a plethora of small journal entries to inflate revenue or reduce expenses, without triggering any analytical procedures being used by the auditors. They may get away with these changes, but their use of randomly-chosen numbers in those journal entries will be spotted in a Benford analysis, since the numbers chosen will not match the Benford distribution. The probability of being detected will increase as the proportion of fraudulent journal entries to the total number of journal entries increases. The risk of detection is increasingly likely if management is pushing to continually increase reported revenue and profits over time, so that more and more fraudulent journal entries are needed to arrive at the required financial results.

It is important to understand the situations to which Benford's Law can be applied. The frequency distribution only occurs for naturally occurring numbers. In a business, examples of these numbers are:

- Journal entries
- The grand total billed on an invoice
- The compiled cost of a product
- The number of units in stock

- The balance in a customer account
- The balance due to a supplier

It does not apply in situations where numbers are assigned, such as a sequentially assigned check number or invoice number. Whenever numbers have a digit pattern that has some meaning (such as a phone number that begins with an assigned area code), a Benford analysis cannot be applied to it.

EXAMPLE

An internal auditor is conducting a Benford analysis of the purchasing records of a business unit, to see if there are any anomalous findings. He finds a spike in the data for purchases beginning with the number 5. Further investigation reveals that the company purchases flowers from the local flower shop for the same amount ($58) every business day, resulting in 260 purchases in the same amount. Because these purchases have such a narrow range of values, they trigger an entirely valid anomaly when compared to the Benford distribution.

Benford's Law is more applicable to larger data sets than to small ones. When the data set contains less than 50 numbers, it is quite possible that the distribution of numbers will differ significantly from what is indicated by Benford's Law, and yet will not be an indicator of fraud. In this situation, the auditor may have to spend a significant amount of time on follow-up testing, reviewing anomalies. Conversely, when the data set is large (perhaps in the tens of thousands), the distribution of numbers should be quite close to the Benford line, so even a small spike in the results is worth investigating.

> **Note:** If the auditor allows a substantial amount of variation from the Benford line, there should be few spikes in the data requiring investigation, which reduces the amount of audit work, but also increases the risk of missing a fraudulent transaction. Conversely, investigating lesser variations from the Benford line will increase the amount of audit work (perhaps substantially), but reduces the risk of not identifying a fraudulent transaction.

Thus far, our main focus has been on applying Benford's Law to the *first* digit in a number. Actually, it can be applied to second and later position numbers as well, on the theory that management likes to round up the numbers in its financial statements. Therefore, there is likely to be a higher incidence of "0" in the second and later position numbers than "9." For example, when management is presented with a revenue figure of $199,999, it is more likely to find a way to round the figure up to $200,000, on the theory that doing so conveys a larger measure of size, even though the incremental increase is actually quite small. The same finding applies to the reporting of earnings per share, where (for example) a controller might be tempted to find ways to increase an initial earnings per share figure of $1.98 to $2.00; this slight increase might have a significant impact on analyst expectations, which drives the motivation of the controller to make the change. In short, this finding can be useful for locating instances of financial statement fraud.

EXAMPLE

Pensive Corporation went public five years ago. Since then, the company has issued 20 quarterly financial statements (including year-end financials), in which 16 of the reported revenue figures had a zero as the second digit. Since the odds of a business reporting a zero 16 times out of 20 strains one's credulity, it seems likely that management has been striving to report revenue figures that exceed psychological thresholds[2], such as sales figures of $50 million, $60 million, and $70 million.

> **Note:** An interesting analysis would be to see if a publicly-held company never reports earnings per share figures with a "4" in the tenths of a cent position. This would mean that the accounting department is creating entries to increase the figure to a "5," which can then be rounded up in the reported amount of earnings per share. For example, a value of $1.194 would be rounded *down* to $1.19 per share, while a value of $1.195 would be rounded *up* to $1.20 per share.

The preceding example might make it look as though Benford's Law can be used to locate all kinds of fraud in short order. This is not really the case. Instead, the analysis works only if the analysis team drills down deeply enough into the data to locate a potentially fraudulent situation. Another concern is that this technique only indicates the possible existence of fraud; someone still needs to find out exactly how fraud is being perpetrated, which calls for a significant amount of additional investigatory work.

Cross-Matching Analysis

Cross-matching analysis involves matching information from different parts of the company to find a match that could point toward a fraud situation. Common examples are:

- Matching employee addresses to the addresses of suppliers, to see if employees have set up dummy entities that are billing the company.
- Matching employee bank accounts to supplier bank accounts, for the same reason just noted.
- Matching employee bank accounts to the bank accounts of other employees, to see if any fake ("ghost") employees have been created, to which payments are being sent.

---

[2] Amounts just below a psychological threshold are usually considered to be significantly smaller than the amounts just over the threshold.

- Matching invoices received to the purchase order database, to detect invoices that were not authorized by a purchase order.
- Matching invoices received to receiving reports, to see if there is no record of receipt of certain billed items.

The analysis can also involve any number of analyses *within* a single data set to search for anomalies. For example:

- Duplicate invoice numbers submitted by the same supplier
- Sequential invoice numbers submitted by the same supplier
- Multiple invoices submitted by a supplier that contain the same billing description
- Equipment charges associated with a contract when no labor hours were charged

Policy Threshold Analysis

A business may have accounting policies in place that impose barriers to some transactions once a certain threshold is reached. A classic example is the corporate purchasing card, with which many organizations do not allow their employees to make purchases above a certain amount, such as $2,000. An easy analysis is to load the individual purchasing card transaction totals into Excel, and run a histogram analysis that will highlight any transactions exceeding the policy threshold. A *histogram* is a diagram consisting of rectangles whose area is proportional to the frequency of a variable and whose width is equal to the class interval. For example, the following histogram was constructed using the Insert >> Charts >> Histogram function in Excel, using a sample set of 30 purchasing card transactions. The histogram shows the distribution of purchases made, where the policy threshold is $2,000 (indicated by a vertical gray line). There are two points of interest in this histogram. One is the presence of several transactions exceeding the threshold (noted with red arrows), which are indicators of policy breaches, though not necessarily of fraud. The other point is a potential breach of purchasing policy, which is the spike in purchases just underneath the policy threshold (noted with a green arrow). The details of the transactions in this anomaly should be investigated to see if larger purchases were split into smaller pieces to keep them underneath the threshold.

Histogram of Purchasing Transactions

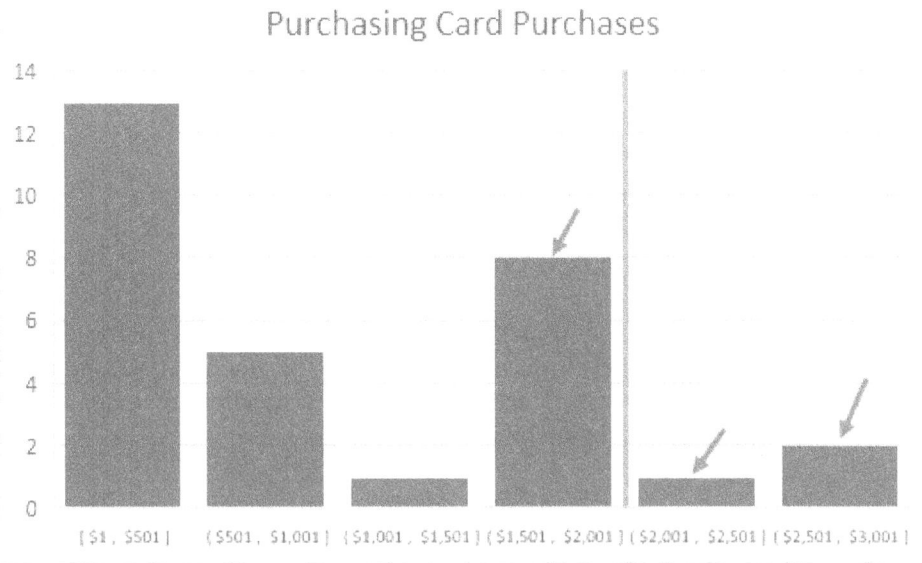

Purchasing Card Purchases

As another example, one could review the volume of credits granted to customers just below the policy threshold that requires a manager's written approval. When there is a spike in the credit volume just below this threshold, a possible reason is that employees are granting credits to friends and family, or are taking kickbacks from customers in exchange for the issuance of credits. Here are several additional policy thresholds to be aware of:

- *Receipt policies*. There may be a spike in reported expenses just below the policy threshold for reimbursement documentation (such as requiring a receipt for expenses exceeding $25). This could be an indicator of excessive claims. Tracking these instances by employee may uncover a few people who routinely submit excessive reimbursement claims.
- *Approval policies*. There may be a spike just below any approval authorization levels, such as $100 for an expense report or $500 for the purchase of a plane ticket, indicating the expenditures are being maximized to just below the tolerable thresholds.
- *Reporting policies*. There may be a spike in any reported figure just below the point at which a report must be filled out, such as having to submit documentation for why obsolete inventory items exceeding a carrying amount of $1,000 can be dispositioned.

In short, a prime source of data for fraud analysis is the pool of transactions occurring just underneath any policy threshold.

Outlier Analysis

An outlier is a value that differs significantly from the other values in a set of data. Data analysis can be used to focus on outliers, which are sometimes associated with fraudulent activity. Examples of activities that could be the focus of an outlier activities analysis are:

- Unusually large price increases by a supplier
- Unusually large cost overruns on supplier contracts
- Unusually large numbers of goods returned to a supplier
- Unusually large overtime payments

The main issue with the analysis of outliers is deciding when a data point is really an outlier, or falls within the main cluster of values. To do this, the auditor compiles a z-score, which is a statistical measurement of a data point's relationship to the mean of a set of data points. The calculation of the z-score is:

$$\frac{(Value - Mean)}{Standard\ deviation}$$

A z-score of zero indicates that the score of a specific value is the same as the mean of the data set to which it is related; such a score is certainly not an outlier. As the score becomes larger (either negative or positive), the related value is more likely to be considered an outlier. A score of one indicates one full standard deviation from the mean, while a score of two represents two standard deviations from the mean, and so forth. Each incremental standard deviation represents the following values:

- 68.2% of all values lie within one standard deviation
- 95.4% of all values lie within two standard deviations
- 99.6% of all values lie within three standard deviations

Thus, a z-score that is approaching two should certainly draw the attention of a fraud auditor, while a z-score of three or more will raise a considerable red flag.

EXAMPLE

An auditor is searching for outlier transactions in a downloaded data set for office supplies. The mean value of a purchase in this data set is $40.79, and the standard deviation from this amount is $26.30. One of the purchases in the data set is for $104.38. Its z-score is calculated as follows:

($104.38 - $40.79) ÷ $26.30 = 2.42

This score is 2.4 standard deviations from the mean, and so could be flagged for further investigation as an outlier.

The standard deviation and mean are easily calculated in Excel. In the following exhibit, we show a data set of 10 numbers, from which the standard deviation and mean are calculated, using the formulas stated in the exhibit.

Calculation of Standard Deviation and Mean

	A	B	C	D	E	F
1						
2		Data				
3		45.27		Standard Deviation	19.53778 =STDEV(B3:B12)	
4		72.85		Mean	45.394 =SUM(C3:C12)/COUNT(C3:C12)	
5		23.99				
6		21.43				
7		18.95				
8		38.09				
9		47.71				
10		56.02				
11		68.28				
12		61.35				

Outlier analysis can also be conducted more simply, by plotting data points on a chart. The concept is addressed in the following example.

EXAMPLE

An internal auditor wants to assess the risk that a business unit has incorrectly billed its customers. This entity manufactures plumbing fixtures, which are sold to retailers. The business grants varying discounts to these retailers, based on the number of units sold to them. In general, it grants a 30% discount, with variations of no more than 5% above and below this value, based on its stated pricing structure. To test whether this is actually the case, the auditor extracts all billing transactions from the firm's database for the past year, and compares the billed prices to the standard prices for each product, resulting in a calculated discount rate. The outcome appears in the following discount rates analysis, where the red arrows highlight three instances in which billings involved either unusually high or low discounts from the standard prices. The auditor decides to investigate all three of these billings in more detail, to ascertain the reasons for the unusual discounts.

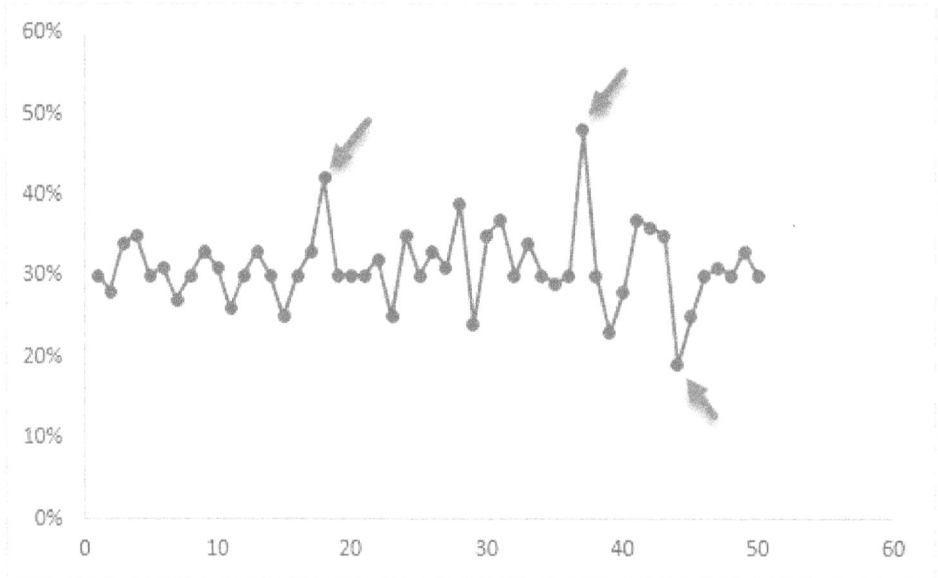

Trend Analysis

Many types of fraud can be found by examining a trend line of data over a period of time. For example, when a purchasing agent starts taking kickbacks from a supplier in exchange for buying too expensive goods, the unit cost paid to that supplier should jump when the kickback begins, and remain high thereafter. A variation on the concept is to generate a trend analysis of raw material returns; if the quantity of returns increases and then stays at a higher level, a kickback situation could have been entered into, where the price remains the same but the supplier is allowed to ship lower-quality goods. Here are several other situations in which trend analysis could be used:

- Trend line of labor rates charged by a contractor, where the rate of price increases exceeds the inflation rate.
- Trend line of equipment rental rates charged by a supplier, where the rate of price increases exceeds the inflation rate.
- Trend line of price increases by a supplier for raw materials and components, where the rate of price increases exceeds the inflation rate.
- Trend line of the ratio of selling price to shipping charges, where an increasing proportion of shipping charges indicates that the supplier may be taking advantage of the company's weak shipping charge monitoring controls.
- Trend line of the cost of goods sold, where an increasing trend shows that sales may be under-reported or that goods are being stolen from the warehouse.

A sample trend analysis appears in the following exhibit, which states the trend line of foodstuffs missing from a grocery store warehouse. The amount missing is derived from a comparison of the book balance of units on hand to the amounts actually counted as part of an ongoing cycle counting program.

Trend Line of Warehouse Losses by Week

Warehouse Losses

$3,000	
$2,500	
$2,000	
$1,500	
$1,000	
$500	
$-	

Week 1, Week 2, Week 3, Week 4, Week 5, Week 6, Week 7, Week 8, Week 9, Week 10, Week 11, Week 12

The exhibit shows a gradual increase in the amount of losses, as the perpetrator waits to see if anyone spots the issue, and then becomes more emboldened over time. The complete absence of losses during weeks 6 and 7 coincides with the arrival of an audit team, which conducts a standard set of audit procedures in the warehouse. Once they leave, the fraud begins again, except at a higher level as the perpetrator becomes bolder.

Round Numbers Analysis

The data can be sorted to search for large round numbers. This is especially useful in an analysis of accounts payable information, where such numbers tend to be indicators of unusual transactions, such as donations to favored charities, contract advances, personal advances, and bribes. These payments are more likely to be discretionary payments by senior management. Most of them will be entirely legitimate, but a few could indicate fraudulent activity.

An example of round numbers fraud is the use of a company purchasing card by an employee to purchase gift cards for personal use. These cards are always in rounded amounts, such as $25, $50, or $100. A specific search for these amounts in an extract of purchasing card data could identify the gift card purchases.

An example of both a round numbers analysis and the avoidance of a policy threshold is when a bank customer repeatedly deposits cash in the amount of $9,900. This is done in order to avoid the bank's legal requirement to report cash deposits to the federal government of at least $10,000, and also because illicit deposits relating to narcotics, money laundering, and so forth tend to be in $100 bills. Thus, sorting on deposit totals and specifically targeting this amount will likely highlight illegal activities.

Round numbers are an indicator of fraudulent activities, but they can also be the result of negotiated prices. For example, a product sells for $8.15 per unit, but a customer negotiates the seller down to $8.00 per unit if it buys 10,000 units. Similarly, a used-car dealership lists the price of a used car at $28,749, but is negotiated down to $28,000 by the buyer.

Duplicate Numbers Analysis

The presence of duplicate numbers in a data set can be an indicator of fraud. For example, one might extract the bank account numbers from the employee master file and sort it to see if any account numbers are present more than once. If so, it is possible that someone on the payroll staff has created a ghost employee and is routing additional pay from that account into his or her bank account. However, it could also mean that a husband and wife work for the same company, and are channeling their pay into a joint account.

As another possibility, someone is inflating the amount of inventory on hand in order to increase the ending inventory valuation, which reduces the cost of goods sold and so increases the reported profit level. To do so, he creates a number of fake inventory records to add items to stock. Since he wants to add a large number of small transactions in order to make the scam less obvious, he has to create several hundred transactions. It is likely that he will get lazy during this process and enter the same quantity for a number of the inventory items. This can be spotted by downloading the record of inventory transactions for a certain period of time, sorting it by unit count, and extracting all duplicate unit quantities for further analysis. It would be particularly interesting to see if these duplicate amounts were entered within a short period of time, and by the same user ID – a strong indicator that someone is deliberately altering the inventory records.

A third possibility is to extract from the check register the amount of all checks issued, and sort them in order to spot duplicate amounts. A person engaged in the repetitive fraudulent issuance of checks tends to create checks in the same amount, even if they are issued to different supplier names, so a series of similar amounts (and especially if they are round numbers) is an indicator of fraudulent check issuances, and so is worthy of more detailed investigation.

A variation on the preceding duplicate payment concept is for an accountant to deliberately send a duplicate payment to a supplier, and then ask the supplier to send back the payment on a new check, which the accountant then intercepts and cashes. A duplicate check analysis can spot the existence of this scam, and makes it more obvious if the perpetrator continues to issue duplicate checks to the same set of suppliers.

Of particular interest are duplicate numbers in multiple fields of a record. For example, two purchases in the same amount on the same day from the same corporate purchasing card is a strong indicator that the card holder has authorized a split payment in order to make a purchase that exceeds the maximum authorized purchase for that card. Another example is multiple inventory receipts for the same inventory item into the same storage location, which indicates a possible duplicate entry (not necessarily fraudulent).

Another possibility is duplicate values occurring on the same date within the same data set, but with other information being different. For example, a supplier might be set up under several different vendor numbers within the payables system, which allows for payment of the same invoice to multiple vendor codes at the same time.

Of course, there are naturally-occurring duplicates in many data sets, so the auditor will need to recognize which ones are expected (such as recurring rent payments), and eliminate them from consideration. Another possibility is to only investigate duplicate amounts above a certain dollar threshold, on the grounds that someone committing fraud would not bother to do so in excessively small amounts.

> **Note:** Many accountants assume that their accounts payable systems will automatically reject a duplicate supplier invoice. However, this is not necessarily the case when there are several business units operating separate payables systems. In this situation, the same supplier could be paid multiple times from different systems. In addition, a supplier might be listed under several different vendor codes within the same system, which again raises the possibility of making duplicate payments.

Subset Aggregation Testing

Subsets of data can be aggregated, usually by total dollars or by total transaction count. This can be used to identify a number of issues, such as who charges the most overtime, which suppliers are paid the most, or which employees use their corporate purchasing cards the most. These findings tend to be buried within the much larger volume of transactions within the accounting and operations records, where those engaged in fraud expect to be able to hide their activities. Here are several examples of possible subset aggregations:

- Aggregate purchases by those that did not have a supporting purchase order authorization, and within that subset by size of purchase, to spot large unauthorized transactions.
- Aggregate customer credits by customer, to see if any customers are abusing the firm's returns policy.
- Aggregate customer credits by customer and authorizing employee, to see if any employees might be getting kickbacks in exchange for processing large credits to certain customers.
- Aggregate customer refunds by credit card number. It is possible that employees are refunding customer credits back to their own credit cards.
- Aggregate expense report reimbursements by employee, to see if anyone is abusing the company's travel and entertainment policy.

Growth Spurt Analysis

Those engaged in fraud have a difficult time keeping their schemes down to a reasonable, undetectable level. Instead, they get caught up in a continual cycle of stealing more and more from the business, which results in a growth spurt that can be detected. To spot these situations, the auditor needs to follow these steps:

1. Combine data sets for multiple reporting periods. This can involve some work, especially if the source database was altered during the analysis period.
2. Calculate the percentage rate of growth over the measurement period, retaining only those parties exceeding a minimum threshold growth rate.
3. Drop out of this remaining group any parties for which the increase in dollar terms is small. This step is necessary, since small dollar increases from a minimal base can result in large calculated growth rates, but very small monetary increases.

The remaining parties still appearing in the analysis can then be investigated in more detail.

The reverse situation, where there is a sudden decline, might also be an indicator of fraud. For example, a sudden drop in the amount of royalties being paid by the user of a patent could indicate that the user is deliberately under-reporting its royalties. Similarly, a municipal government might have grounds for suspicion when the room taxes being paid by a local motel suddenly decline.

A growth spurt is not an automatic sign of a fraud scheme. There could be a change in the circumstances of a business that completely justifies the increase. For example, a sudden spurt in the cost of goods sold could be triggered when the product mix changes away from services and towards manufactured goods. Similarly, the holder of a company purchasing card is promoted into a new position that requires extensive travel, so a corresponding jump in travel expenses would be expected.

EXAMPLE

The Slobbering Dog Brewery has been experiencing modest, steady growth for the last 10 years, as its owners slowly expand its distribution area. This has resulted in sales growth of roughly 4% per year. However, the firm's cost of goods sold started increasing at a faster rate three years ago, to the point where Slobbering Dog is generating almost no profits at all. An analysis of the situation reveals that the firm switched to a different supplier of malted barley at that time; this supplier has gradually increased its prices since then. Further investigation reveals that the purchasing manager has never put the malted barley out for bid, even though he has routinely done so for everything else in the company. After hiring a private investigator, the owners determine that the purchasing manager has been receiving kickbacks from the supplier in exchange for approving excessive malted barley prices.

Relative Size Factor Analysis

A relative size factor analysis searches for a subset of data in which the largest amount is significantly larger than the other amounts in the data. It is calculated as the largest record in a subset, divided by the second largest record in the subset. Or,

Largest record value ÷ Second largest value = Relative size factor

For example, a routine analysis of the building maintenance expenditures account reveals that the largest expenditure in the past year was for $20,000, while the second largest expenditure was for only $1,500. The resulting 13.3x relative size factor indicates that the largest expenditure is an exceptional anomaly, and perhaps should have been capitalized as a fixed asset, rather than being charged to expense.

If the relative size factor is fairly close to 1, this indicates the absence of outliers from the data set, and so provides no notable transactions. However, quite a large factor indicates the presence of a transaction that may have been recorded incorrectly, or which indicates a fraud situation. For example, this analysis could identify any of the following:

- An entry mistakenly made without a decimal point. Thus, an invoice for $142.17 could be entered into the payables module as $14,217.
- An incorrect unit of measure on an inventory item translates into a much larger total quantity. Thus, an entry of 100 units that is mislabeled as dozens becomes 1,200 units.
- A subset aggregation test reveals that one accounting clerk is responsible for ten times the number of credits of the clerk with the next-largest number of credits granted, which indicates the existence of a kickback scheme between the clerk and his or her customers.

A variation on the concept is to divide the smallest number in a data set by the average for the set, in order to identify understatements.

Time-Series Analysis

Time-series analysis is used to extrapolate information from a successive series of data points over a period of time. By extending these data points into the future, one can compare them to actual results to search for significant differences between the two values. For example, one could use this analysis to compare actual to forecasted revenues from a retail location. The same approach could be applied to the trend of customer refunds granted, customer coupon redemptions, overtime expenses incurred, and warranty claims submitted by customers. The appearance of a large difference between the two values should trigger an investigation.

> **Note:** A time-series analysis is most useful when the immediate past values are stable, and so can be reasonably extended into the future.

Excel contains a number of tools that are useful for time-series analysis. In the following sub-sections, we describe the uses to which these Excel functions can be put, and provide instructions on how to use them. As the basis for this analysis, we used a series of unit sales for a retail operation, which can be extended into the future and then compared to actual results to see if there are any variances worth exploring further. As we describe each successive Excel function, keep in mind that the key point is to derive a line from the series of past data points that can be used as the basis for predictions of the future.

Moving Averages Function

A moving average calculation generates a forecast based on the most recent historical information. Excel provides a tool that automatically creates a moving average from this data. To use the moving averages function, it is first necessary to download the function into Excel. To do so, select the **File** tab, then **Options**, and then **Add-Ins**. Select the **Analysis Toolpak** to download the analysis functionality into Excel. Once the toolpak is loaded, follow these steps:

1. Enter on an Excel spreadsheet a series of data points relating to the information to be forecasted. A sample appears below.

⊿ A	B	C
1		
2	Period	Unit Sales
3	1	17,400
4	2	16,900
5	3	17,900
6	4	17,400
7	5	18,300
8	6	16,400
9	7	18,500
10	8	17,700

2. Select the **Data** tab and pick the **Data Analysis** option. When the following **Data Analysis** box appears, select the **Moving Average** option and click on **OK**.

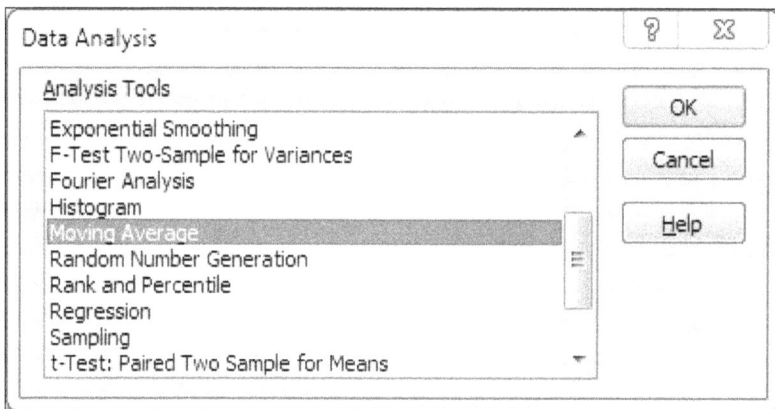

Data Analysis

Analysis Tools

Exponential Smoothing
F-Test Two-Sample for Variances
Fourier Analysis
Histogram
Moving Average
Random Number Generation
Rank and Percentile
Regression
Sampling
t-Test: Paired Two Sample for Means

OK
Cancel
Help

3. The following **Moving Average** box appears. Enter the cell input range (in this case, cells C2 through C10) in the **Input Range**. Enter the cell address

range for the resulting moving average (in this case, cells D3 through D10) in the **Output Range**. The completed Moving Average box follows.

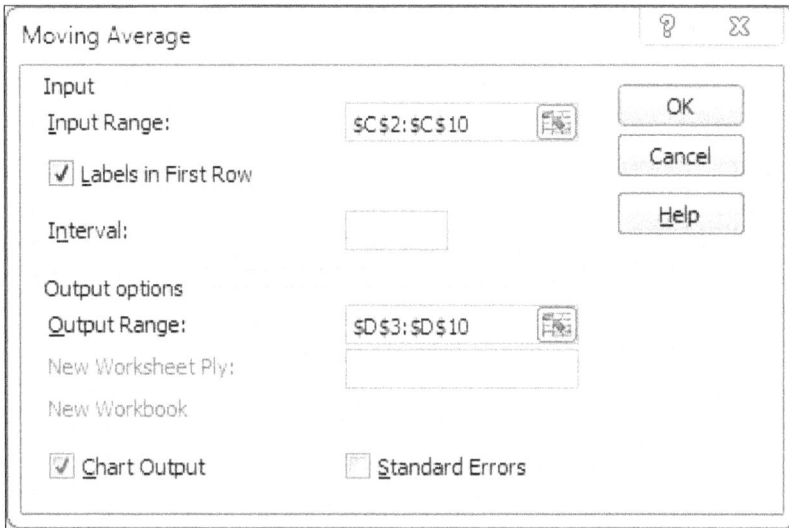

4. Excel automatically creates a moving average based on the listed data, which appears in column D in the following page view, along with a moving average chart. The chart was triggered because we checked the **Chart Output** option in the preceding **Moving Average** box.

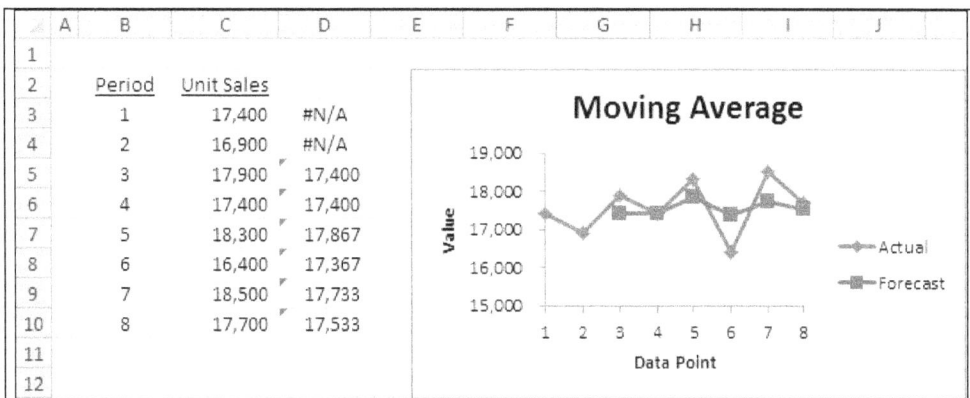

Exponential Smoothing Function

Exponential smoothing is a variation on the preceding moving average concept, where the key difference is the presence of a damping factor in the options that Excel presents. The damping factor is 1 minus the smoothing constant. The smoothing constant determines the level at which actual experience influences a forecast. Thus, if a prior forecast was too high, the smoothing constant is used to reduce the forecast in the next period. Conversely, if a prior forecast was too low, the smoothing constant increases the forecast in the next period. A high damping factor smooths out the peaks and valleys in the data more than a low damping factor.

To use exponential smoothing in Excel, follow the same steps just noted for the moving average function, except you should select the **Exponential Smoothing** option when the **Data Analysis** box appears. Completing the box while using the same data points just noted for the moving average example results in the following entry in the **Exponential Smoothing** box:

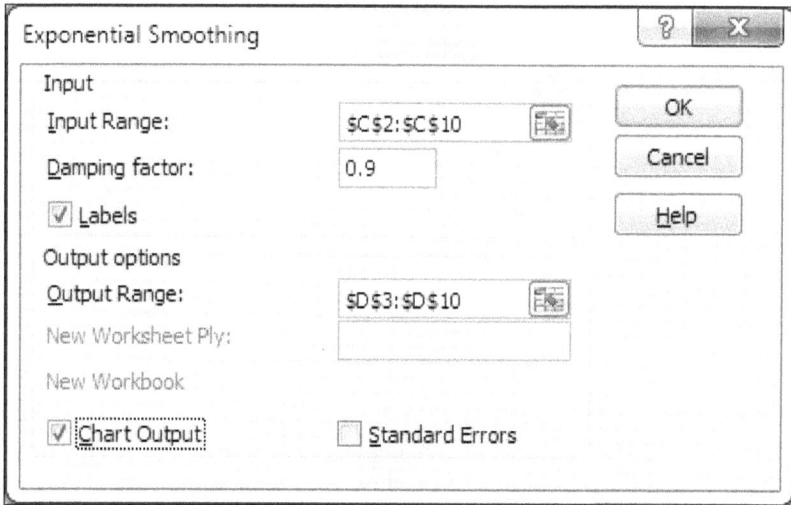

The result of this entry is the following exponential smoothing outcome generated by Excel. Note how the forecast line in the chart is much smoother than was the case with the moving average outcome. This is because the damping factor was set at a high 0.9.

	A	B	C	D
1				
2		Period	Unit Sales	
3		1	17,400	#N/A
4		2	16,900	17,400
5		3	17,900	17,350
6		4	17,400	17,405
7		5	18,300	17,405
8		6	16,400	17,494
9		7	18,500	17,385
10		8	17,700	17,496
11				

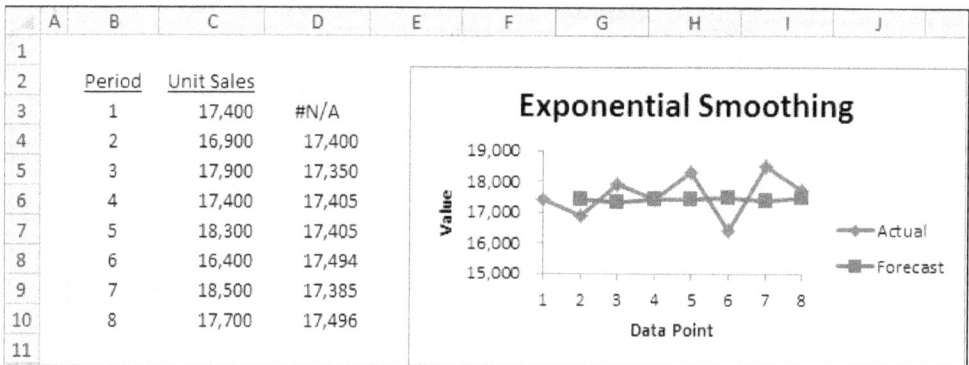

If the damping factor had instead been set at a much lower 0.1, the outcome would have been as follows, where the smoothing follows the historical data much more closely.

	A	B	C	D	E	F	G	H	I	J
1										
2		Period	Unit Sales				Exponential Smoothing			
3		1	17,400	#N/A						
4		2	16,900	17,400						
5		3	17,900	16,950						
6		4	17,400	17,805						
7		5	18,300	17,441						Actual
8		6	16,400	18,214						Forecast
9		7	18,500	16,581						
10		8	17,700	18,308						
11										

Chart "Exponential Smoothing": Value axis 15,000–19,000; Data Point axis 1–8; series Actual and Forecast.

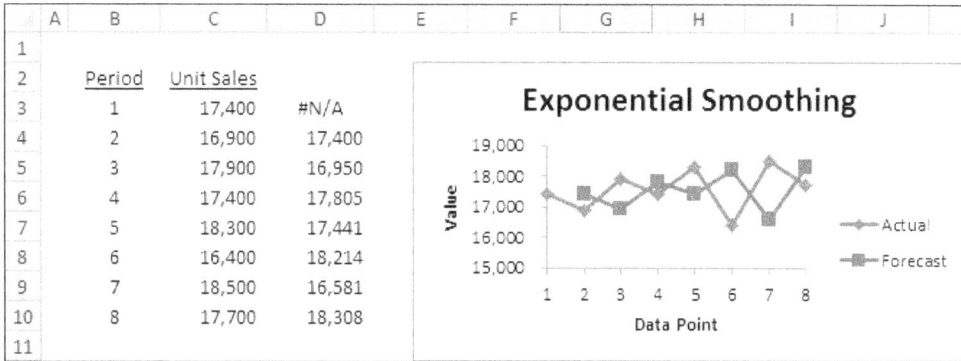

Linear Trend Function

The linear trend function allows one to highlight a set of consecutive numbers and then drag over additional cells. By doing so, Excel automatically calculates the trend associated with the highlighted numbers and extends the trend line into the additional cells. In the following example, the first three (shaded) cells were originally input into a financial model, and then extended with the linear trend function to create the trend appearing in the next three cells.

Trend Line Calculation

Historical Period 1	Historical Period 2	Historical Period 3	Projected Period 1	Projected Period 2	Projected Period 3
5,000	6,200	7,000	8,067	9,067	10,067

The problem with this dragging function is that the linear trend calculation is not re-peated if there is a change in the original data set. Consequently, the drag function is not recommended for high-usage models for which there are expected to be a number of iterations.

An alternative approach is to create a table of all relevant historical values in Ex-cel, plot this information in an Excel chart, and then add a trend line to the chart. The trend line is obtained by right-clicking on the historical data line appearing in the chart and then selecting the "Linear" option. For example, the following time series of data is entered into Excel:

3000, 4500, 3800, 5000, 4300, 6100

The resulting chart is presented in the following exhibit, along with the associated trend line. Also note that Excel has provided the formula for the resulting trend line within the chart, which is:

$$Y = 460x + 2840$$

Sample Plot of Historical Data with Linear Trend Overlay

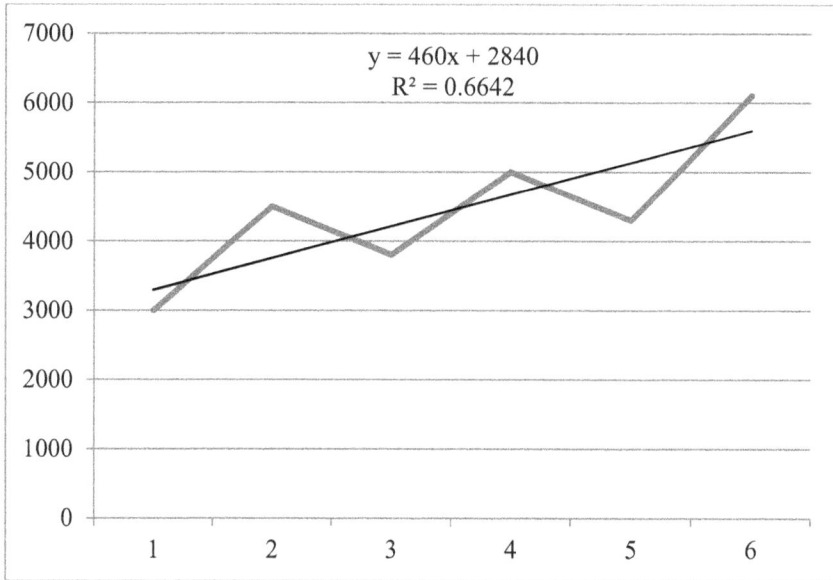

$y = 460x + 2840$
$R^2 = 0.6642$

The chart also notes that the data has an R value of 0.6642. The result of the formula ("r") is a value between negative one and positive one, where a value closer to positive one represents a tight relationship between the dependent and independent variables. As noted in the following exhibit, the 0.6642 value indicates a strong positive relationship between the data and the trend line.

Strength of Correlation Coefficient

R Value	Level of Relationship
Positive 0.70 or higher	Very strong positive relationship
Positive 0.40 – 0.69	Strong positive relationship
Positive 0.30 – 0.39	Moderate positive relationship
Positive 0.20 – 0.29	Weak positive relationship
Positive 0.01 – 0.19	Minimal positive relationship
Zero	No relationship
Negative 0.01 – 0.19	Minimal negative relationship
Negative 0.20 – 0.29	Weak negative relationship
Negative 0.30 – 0.39	Moderate negative relationship
Negative 0.40 – 0.69	Strong negative relationship
Negative 0.70 or lower	Very strong negative relationship

Cubic Volume Analytics

A useful tool in forensic analytics is converting the numbers in a spreadsheet into a cubic volume analysis, to see if they are reasonable. For example, management is overstating the amount of ending inventory in order to report a lower cost of goods sold, thereby artificially increasing profits. The auditor can evaluate the veracity of these ending inventory figures by multiplying the product dimensions data in the item master file by the ending inventory unit counts, to see if the resulting cubic volume could reasonably be expected to fit in the company's warehouse. Another option is to multiply the number of people reported on the company's payroll and its payables register (for contractors) by a reasonable amount of square feet per person (such as 200 square feet), and then comparing this figure to the square footage of the office building in which they are housed. If it does not appear likely to stuff that many people into the assigned space, it is possible that someone is running a ghost employee scheme, making up fake employees in order to pay them and abscond with the resulting paychecks.

Ratio Analysis

Ratio analysis is the comparison of line items in the financial statements of a business. Ratio analysis is used to evaluate a number of issues with an entity, such as its liquidity, efficiency of operations, and profitability. Ratio analysis is particularly useful when employed in the following ways:

- *Trend line*. Calculate each ratio over a large number of reporting periods, to see if there is a trend in the results. The trend can indicate financial difficulties that would not otherwise be apparent if ratios were being examined for a single period. Trend lines can also be used to estimate the direction of future ratio performance.
- *Industry comparison*. Calculate the same ratios for competitors in the same industry, and compare the results across all of the companies reviewed. Since these businesses likely operate with similar fixed asset investments and have similar capital structures, the results of a ratio analysis should be similar. If this is not the case, it can indicate a potential issue.

Ratio analysis is a useful tool. However, there are a number of limitations to be aware of. They are:

- *Historical*. All of the information used in ratio analysis is derived from actual historical results. This does not mean that the same results will carry forward into the future.
- *Aggregation*. The information in a financial statement line item being used for a ratio analysis may have been aggregated differently in the past, so that running the ratio analysis on a trend line does not compare the same information through the entire trend period.
- *Operational changes*. A company may change its underlying operational structure to such an extent that a ratio calculated several years ago and

compared to the same ratio today would yield a misleading conclusion. For example, if a just-in-time production system was implemented, this might lead to a reduced investment in fixed assets, whereas a ratio analysis might conclude that the company is letting its fixed asset base become too old.

- *Accounting policies*. Different companies may have different policies for recording the same accounting transaction. This means that comparing the ratio results of different companies may be like comparing apples and oranges. For example, one company might use accelerated depreciation while another company uses straight line depreciation, or one company records a sale at gross while the other company does so at net.
- *Business conditions*. Place ratio analysis in the context of the general business environment. For example, 60 days of sales outstanding might be considered poor in a period of rapidly growing sales, but might be excellent during an economic contraction when customers are in severe financial condition and unable to pay their bills.
- *Interpretation*. It can be quite difficult to ascertain the reason for the results of a ratio. For example, a current ratio of 2:1 might appear to be excellent, until it becomes apparent that the company just sold a large amount of its stock to bolster its cash position. A more detailed analysis might reveal that the current ratio will only temporarily be at that level, and will probably decline in the near future.
- *Company strategy*. It can be dangerous to conduct a ratio analysis comparison between two firms that are pursuing different strategies. For example, one company may be following a low-cost strategy, and so is willing to accept a lower gross margin in exchange for more market share. Conversely, a company in the same industry is focusing on a high customer service strategy where its prices are higher and gross margins are higher, but it will never attain the revenue levels of the first company.
- *Point in time*. Some ratios extract information from the balance sheet. Be aware that the information on the balance sheet is only as of the last day of the reporting period. If there was an unusual spike or decline in the account balance on the last day of the reporting period, this can impact the outcome of the ratio analysis.

In short, ratio analysis has a variety of limitations. However, as long as the auditor is aware of these problems and uses alternative and supplemental methods to collect and interpret information, ratio analysis is still useful.

Supplier-Specific Analytics

We have provided a number of examples in the preceding pages that refer to problems relating to payables. In this section, we highlight several topics that are more specifically targeted at suppliers.

Adjacent Supplier Analysis

A reasonable analysis is to calculate the distance of all suppliers from the corporate headquarters, especially those that have post office box addresses. The intent is to spot any instances in which an employee could authorize a payment to a fake company, and then walk or drive to the receiving location in order to collect the payment. To save time, the analysis could eliminate all suppliers to whom minimal payments were made.

Supplier Decline Analysis

One of the more common trends seen in fraud cases is that the person committing fraud tends to keep increasing the size of the fraud over time. This can present a problem when the person wants to retire or leave the business for some other reason, since the ascending path of the fraud suddenly vanishes. This presents an occasional opportunity for the auditor, who can run a periodic analysis about why some suppliers have stopped billing the company, or some customers have stopped demanding credits, or some employees are no longer on the payroll. Only the canniest fraudster will gradually reduce his or her activities down to zero prior to leaving the company. Instead, there is usually a sudden decline in expenditures (and increase in profits) that is well worth investigating. One possibility is to cross-check who has left the accounting department around the time when these spending declines also occur.

Supplier Predictors of Fraud

An analysis of suppliers to spot instances of fraud could use a data download from the vendor master file and payables register to search for the following issues. When several of the indicated issues arise, this represents an increased risk of fraud:

- *No purchase orders.* The invoices being issued do not reference an authorizing purchase order, indicating that the supplier is not working through the purchasing department.
- *Services orientation.* The provision of services to a company, such as legal advice, equipment maintenance, and lawn care, are more difficult to prove, and also do not require a receiving report.
- *Social security identification.* When a supplier uses a social security number on its Form W-9, this indicates that the entity is more informal, and probably involves only one person.
- *Under authorization threshold.* The supplier routinely issues invoices for amounts that are just under the threshold at which formal authorization is required for supplier invoices.

Dealing with False Positives

When engaged in a forensic analytics inquiry, a major concern is the presence of false positives, where the analysis indicates the presence of fraud when that is not really the case. Investigating large numbers of false positives can soak up a large part of an auditor's budgeted time, to the point where the entire process is rendered uneconomical. When this situation arises, consider taking the following actions:

1. Evaluate whether the test was appropriately planned and performed. This might require several iterations before the number of notable items has been reduced to a reasonable number.
2. Sort the remaining notable items into groups by common characteristics. Sampling a few items from each group may establish whether there is a real risk of fraud within that group, or whether they can be safely ignored.

Summary

The techniques discussed in this book are not a sure-fire way to spot fraudulent transactions and errors. Rather, they can be used to spot records that are more likely to indicate fraudulent behavior or other problems, which can then be investigated in more detail. Thus, forensic analytics is really a two-stage approach, where software tools are used to extract anomalies from large data sets, and in-person inquiries are then employed to investigate those anomalies in more detail. It is also a useful backstop for detective and preventive controls, since it adds another technique for spotting issues that might otherwise fall between the cracks of a typical system of controls.

Glossary

B

Benford's Law. The concept that, in a naturally occurring set of numbers, smaller digits appear disproportionately more often as the leading digits.

C

Concatenation. The joining of character strings end-to-end.

E

Exponential smoothing. A method for assigning exponentially decreasing weights for newest to oldest observations, so that less priority is given to older observations.

F

False positive. A result indicating that a given condition is present when it is not.

Forensic analytics. A set of techniques used to discover patterns in a data set that can pinpoint the presence of fraudulent transactions and errors.

H

Histogram. A diagram consisting of rectangles whose area is proportional to the frequency of a variable and whose width is equal to the class interval.

Horizontal analysis. The comparison of historical financial information over a series of reporting periods.

M

Mean. The average of a set of numerical values.

O

Occupational fraud. When employees misuse or divert their employer's assets for personal gain.

S

Standard deviation. A measure of the amount of variation or dispersion of a set of values.

Z

Z-score. A statistical measurement of a data point's relationship to the mean of a set of data points.

Index